Congressional
Research
Service

Israel: Possible Military Strike Against Iran's Nuclear Facilities

Jim Zanotti, Coordinator
Specialist in Middle Eastern Affairs

Kenneth Katzman
Specialist in Middle Eastern Affairs

Jeremiah Gertler
Specialist in Military Aviation

Steven A. Hildreth
Specialist in Missile Defense

September 28, 2012

Congressional Research Service

7-5700

www.crs.gov

R42443

Summary

Several published reports indicate that top Israeli decisionmakers are seriously considering whether to order a military strike on Iran's nuclear facilities, and if so, when. Twice in Israel's history, it has conducted air strikes aimed at halting or delaying what Israeli policymakers believed to be efforts to acquire nuclear weapons by a Middle Eastern state—destroying Iraq's Osirak reactor in 1981 and a facility the Israelis identified as a reactor under construction in Syria in 2007. Today, Israeli officials generally view the prospect of a nuclear-armed Iran as an unacceptable threat to Israeli security—with some describing it as an existential threat. This report analyzes key factors that may influence Israeli political decisions relating to a possible strike on Iranian nuclear facilities. These include, but are not limited to, the views of and relationships among Israeli leaders; the views of the Israeli public; U.S., regional, and international stances and responses as perceived and anticipated by Israel; Israeli estimates of the potential effectiveness and risks of a possible strike; and responses Israeli leaders anticipate from Iran and Iranian-allied actors—including Hezbollah and Hamas—regionally and internationally.

For Congress, the potential impact—short- and long-term—of an Israeli decision regarding Iran and its implementation is a critical issue of concern. By all accounts, such an attack could have considerable regional and global security, political, and economic repercussions, not least for the United States, Israel, and their bilateral relationship. It is unclear what the ultimate effect of a strike would be on the likelihood of Iran acquiring nuclear weapons. The current Israeli government, President Barack Obama, and many Members of Congress have similar concerns about Iran's nuclear program. They appear to have a range of views on how best to address those shared concerns. Iran maintains that its nuclear program is solely for peaceful, civilian energy and research purposes, and U.S. intelligence assessments say that Iran has not made a decision to build nuclear weapons. However, Iran continues to enrich uranium in militarily hardened sites and questions remain about its nuclear weapons capabilities and intentions.

Short- and long-term questions for Members of Congress to consider regarding a possible Israeli decision to strike Iranian nuclear facilities militarily might include, but are not limited to, the following:

- How might an Israeli strike affect options and debate regarding short-term and long-term U.S. relations and security cooperation with, and foreign assistance to, Israel and other regional countries?

- Would an Israeli strike be considered self-defense? Why or why not? What would be the legal and policy implications either way?

- How might a strike affect the implementation of existing sanctions legislation on Iran or options and debate over new legislation on the subject?

- How might Congress consult with the Obama Administration on and provide oversight with respect to various political and military options?

This report has many aspects that are the subject of vigorous debate and remain fully or partially outside public knowledge. CRS does not claim to independently confirm any sources cited within this report that attribute specific positions or views to various Israeli, U.S., or other officials.

This is an update of a report dated March 28, 2012. However, the only updated material is the initial section entitled "Developments from Late March to September 2012."

Contents

Figures

Contacts

Developments From Late March to September 2012

Many media reports in Israel, the United States, and elsewhere since late March 2012—and especially since August—have focused closely on apparent differences between the Netanyahu government in Israel and the Obama Administration on potential "red lines" for possible military action. After seemingly unsuccessful attempts by Israeli Prime Minister Binyamin Netanyahu to persuade President Barack Obama to present Iran with a time-specific ultimatum (see "U.S. Concerns and Possible Responses: Possible Impact on Israeli Decisionmaking" below), prospects for future Israeli military action remain unclear. The complex array of information and views set forth in this section may help U.S. policymakers address relevant questions on this issue within the context of various regional and global economic, political, and security concerns.

As with other parts of the report, this section has many elements that are the subject of vigorous debate and remain fully or partially outside public knowledge. CRS does not claim that it has confirmed independently any sources cited within this report that attribute specific positions or views to Israeli, U.S., or other officials.

Issue Status: Possible Israeli Decision and Public Debate

Israeli and international media reports have continued speculating that Israeli Prime Minister Binyamin Netanyahu may order an Israeli military attack on Iranian nuclear facilities in the coming months. The rationale for a possible strike is set forth in detail below (see "Possible "Zone of Immunity" and Israel's Ability to Act Independently"). This has enlivened an already vigorous public debate in Israel (as discussed below). A wide array of current and former leaders in Israel's political, military, and security establishments have either publicly expressed opposition or are reportedly opposed, not to an attack in principle, but to an attack without U.S. support given possible operational and political fallout.[1] Seemingly heated private and public exchanges between the Obama Administration and Netanyahu government (discussed below) have occurred within the context of frequent consultations—including summer 2012 visits to Israel by Secretary of State Hillary Clinton, Secretary of Defense Leon Panetta, and National Security Advisor Tom Donilon.

In a September 27 speech before the United Nations General Assembly in which he stressed that the hour was getting "very late," Netanyahu said, "I believe that faced with a clear red line, Iran will back down. This will give more time for sanctions and diplomacy to convince Iran to dismantle its nuclear weapons program altogether." He asserted that otherwise, at current rates of uranium enrichment, Iran could reach the final stage of enrichment by the spring or summer of 2013.[2] Netanyahu's remarks appear to have convinced several former Israeli officials and other international commentators that the timeline for a possible Israeli attack has been pushed back at least to early 2013.[3] However, one Israeli journalist reportedly wrote, "If one takes his statements

---

[1] See, e.g., David Remnick, "The Vegetarian," *New Yorker*, September 3, 2012.

[2] http://www.haaretz.com/news/diplomacy-defense/netanyahu-faced-with-clear-red-line-iran-will-back-down-on-nuclear-program.premium-1.466987

[3] Dan Margalit, "A sigh of relief at the White House," *Israel Hayom*, September 28, 2012; Dan Williams, "Israelis see no Iran war this year after Netanyahu's speech," *Reuters*, September 28, 2012; Jay Solomon, "Netanyahu Demands 'Red Line' on Iran," *Wall Street Journal*, September 28, 2012.

seriously, within a short time, months at most, if Iran is not deterred and if the US does not attack, Israel will launch an attack on its own."[4]

Speculation persists regarding a possible Israeli strike, even though—as discussed below (see "Effect on Iran's Nuclear Program")—most Israeli officials and analysts agree that military action might only delay, not destroy, Iran's nuclear program. Other efforts—diplomacy, sanctions, reported covert action, even implied threats of military action by Israel or the United States—have not led Iran's regime either to stop expanding its uranium enrichment activities or to take steps toward assuring the international community that its nuclear program is confined to purely peaceful purposes. Israel is not a direct party to the P5+1 (see "Military Action Versus Alternative Courses of Action" below for a definition of this term) negotiations over Iran's nuclear program, where technical discussions that continued in the spring and summer of 2012 made no apparent progress.[5]

In August 2012, Israeli Deputy Foreign Minister Danny Ayalon called upon the international community to acknowledge that diplomacy had failed.[6] In August 2012, Congress and the President enacted the Iran Threat Reduction and Syria Human Rights Act of 2012 (P.L. 112-158), an additional sanctions law aimed at Iran's oil exports.[7] Most analysts agree that these sanctions, combined with preexisting U.S. and international sanctions (see "Military Action Versus Alternative Courses of Action" below), are significantly affecting Iran's economy, and reports indicate that Israeli officials may seek additional sanctions.[8] The August 2012 International Atomic Energy Agency (IAEA) report on Iran's nuclear program reiterated concern over continued enrichment and evidence of possible military dimensions to the program.[9] For more information on U.S. and international sanctions, diplomatic efforts, and their collective impact, as well as the August IAEA report, see CRS Report RL32048, *Iran: U.S. Concerns and Policy Responses*, by Kenneth Katzman; CRS Report RS20871, *Iran Sanctions*, by Kenneth Katzman; and CRS Report R40094, *Iran's Nuclear Program: Tehran's Compliance with International Obligations*, by Paul K. Kerr.

Israeli concerns regarding a potential Iranian nuclear weapons capability may be exacerbated by reports that Iran has deliberately provided faulty information about its nuclear program to international monitors.[10] This may further heighten Israeli and international concerns about the reliability and comprehensiveness of current information regarding the program and its progress.

Media attention to deliberations among Netanyahu and the other members of the 14-member Israeli security cabinet (see "Decisionmakers: Views and Interactions" below) has intensified. A vote of approval from the security cabinet is necessary before ordering military action. A late August *New York Times* report indicated that of those within the security cabinet whose views are

---

[4] Nahum Barnea, quoted in Harriet Sherwood, "Binyamin Netanyahu's UN bomb triggers derision and admiration," *guardian.co.uk*, September 28, 2012.

[5] For a discussion of Israel's reported positions regarding negotiations, see Gareth Porter, "U.S.-Israel Deal to Demand Qom Closure Threatens Nuclear Talks," *InterPress Service*, April 12, 2012.

[6] Jodi Rudoren, "Israeli Minister Asks Nations to Say Iran Talks Have Failed," *New York Times*, August 12, 2012.

[7] CRS Report RS20871, *Iran Sanctions*, by Kenneth Katzman.

[8] Isabel Kershner, "Israeli Foreign Ministry Calls for More Sanctions on Iran," *nytimes.com*, September 27, 2012.

[9] IAEA, *Implementation of the NPT Safeguards Agreement and relevant provisions of Security Council resolutions in the Islamic Republic of Iran*, August 2012.

[10] Stuart Winer, "Iran admits it deceived the West over nuclear program," *Times of Israel*, September 20, 2012.

thought to be known, approximately six members are in favor of a strike, with three or four opposed.[11]

The implications for Israeli decisionmaking of press articles pointing to Israeli emphasis on home front safety[12] and streamlined cabinet procedures reportedly giving Netanyahu greater control over the decisionmaking process[13] are unclear. In August 2012, Netanyahu appointed Avi Dichter, a former head of the Israel Security Agency (also known as the Shin Bet), as Home Front Defense Minister after his predecessor was named ambassador to China. Reports indicate that Dichter—though not a member of the security cabinet—has joined the group of eight other ministers (previously known as the "octet," now known as the "group of nine") that has particularly significant influence over the national security decisionmaking process.[14] Netanyahu disbanded security cabinet meetings earlier than planned during the first week of September, reportedly due to leaks of disagreements over when Iran would reach a "zone of immunity" (the term is described below—see "Possible "Zone of Immunity" and Israel's Ability to Act Independently").[15] If, when, and how Netanyahu might call a vote in the security cabinet and/or the full 29-member cabinet remains unclear.[16]

Another possible consideration for Netanyahu is that he will face national elections sometime in 2013; he has faced a drop in approval ratings in 2012—from over 50% in March to 31% in August.[17] This drop may not fundamentally undermine Netanyahu's chances for another prime ministerial term in Israel's coalition-based parliamentary system. However, changing electoral prospects might affect his and other actors' decisionmaking on Iran.[18] Polls continue to indicate that a majority of Israelis opposes a unilateral Israeli strike against Iranian nuclear facilities at this time, but that a slight majority would support a joint U.S.-Israel strike.[19] Ehud Olmert, Israel's previous prime minister, who reportedly ordered Israel's 2007 strike on a presumed Syrian

---

[11] Rudoren and Sanger, op. cit. A September bulletin from a Washington, DC-based consulting firm asserted a slight numerical edge within the security cabinet for those opposing a strike, with four (including Defense Minister Ehud Barak) listed as "unknown" or "uncertain." Nathaniel Kern and Matthew M. Reed, "Netanyahu's Divided Cabinet," *Foreign Reports Bulletin*, September 19, 2012. Reports have focused on possible changes in the position of Barak, one of the primary public exponents of a possible Israeli strike, as well as the views of Vice Prime Minister and Minister for Strategic Affairs Moshe Ya'alon. See Yossi Verter, "Reshuffling the deck: Barak now opposes Israeli strike on Iran, sources say," *Ha'aretz*, September 7, 2012; Hagai Golan and Stella Korin-Lieber, "Barak: I see eye-to-eye with Netanyahu on Iran," *Globes*, September 13, 2012; Ari Shavit, "IDF chief of staff-turned-vice premier: 'We are not bluffing,'" *Ha'aretz Magazine*, June 14, 2012; Remnick, op. cit.

[12] Calev Ben-David and Gwen Ackerman, "Israel to Hold Home Front Drill Amid Rise in Iran Tensions," *Bloomberg*, August 12, 2012.

[13] Attila Somfalvi, "Revised gov't protocol gives PM unprecedented powers," *ynetnews.com*, August 12, 2012.

[14] Herb Keinon, "Security cabinet remains key in deciding on war," *jpost.com*, September 6, 2012.

[15] "Citing leak, Netanyahu disbands security cabinet meeting," *Jewish Telegraphic Agency*, September 5, 2012.

[16] Keinon, op. cit. A September 2012 *New Yorker* article on Israel's 2007 strike on the presumed Al Kibar reactor in Syria discusses how security cabinet deliberations proceeded in that case. David Makovsky, "The Silent Strike," *New Yorker*, September 17, 2012.

[17] "Netanyahu Approval," jewishjournal.com/rosnersdomain.

[18] See, e.g., Yossi Verter, "In UN speech, Netanyahu pitches Iran as key selling point for early Israeli elections," *haaretz.com*, September 28, 2012.

[19] http://www.pcpsr.org/survey/polls/2012/p45ejoint html. This poll was taken on September 9-14, 2012 and has a margin of error of 4.5%. It was conducted jointly by the Harry S. Truman Research Institute for the Advancement of Peace at the Hebrew University of Jerusalem and the Palestinian Center for Policy and Survey Research in Ramallah. The poll was supported by the Ford Foundation Cairo office and the Konrad Adenauer Stiftung in Ramallah and Jerusalem. See Remnick, op. cit., for a discussion of the possible impact of polls on Netanyahu's decisionmaking.

nuclear reactor, and whose political comeback prospects have been the subject of Israeli domestic speculation,[20] was quoted as saying in September:

> Worse comes to worst, and all options have been tried, then, naturally it may force Israel to act to defend its existence. But it must be clear that we tried with the international community, and particularly with the United States, to act together before we resort to the last option of an Israeli military operation.[21]

Public debate in Israel continues to reflect disagreement over both the likelihood and the advisability of an attack. At least one analyst has asserted that Israeli leaders appear to be preparing the "Israeli home front, and international public opinion, for the inevitably messy aftermath of any such action."[22] Other commentators—who note that Israeli leaders did not provide prior warning before military attacks in 1981 and 2007, respectively, against presumed Iraqi and Syrian nuclear reactors—have said that "all the loose talk of a brewing strike is a signal the warnings are little more than posturing."[23] One journalist argued that Israel might strike Iran "just to prove that they're serious" to a largely skeptical world.[24] Another journalist wrote that the key question "is whether Netanyahu sees the threat of Iran building a nuclear bomb as so severe that he is willing to risk severe friction with the United States, a severe blow to the Israeli economy, the possibility of a bloody regional war, and a hail of missiles from Iran, Hezbollah, Hamas, and perhaps Syria hitting Israel."[25]

Possible Operational and Cost-Benefit Considerations for Israel

Israeli censorship rules reportedly limit public discussion of operational details of a possible Israeli strike on Iranian nuclear facilities. Nevertheless, sources that discuss potential military capabilities, options, and outcomes, such as a 2012 book by an Israeli military correspondent and an Israeli military historian,[26] could shed some light on Israeli decisionmakers' calculations. U.S. and international sources have provided some additional information on this subject since late March 2012.[27] A September report from the Center for Strategic and International Studies (CSIS) concluded that although an Israeli strike was possible, "it would be complex and high risk in the operational level and would lack any assurances of a high mission success rate." Furthermore, the report stated that Iranian retaliation will have "devastating regional consequences."[28] Some other

---

[20] Isabel Kershner, "Former Israeli Premier Gets Suspended Sentence," *New York Times*, September 24, 2012.

[21] Makovsky, op. cit.

[22] Oren Kessler, "The Decider," *foreignpolicy.com*, August 23, 2012, citing views attributed to Uzi Rabi, director of the Moshe Dayan Center for Middle Eastern Studies at Tel Aviv University.

[23] Ibid., citing Israeli journalists Motti Kirshenbaum and Ben Caspit.

[24] Ben Caspit, quoted in Rudoren, op. cit.

[25] Yossi Melman, "Israel May Have Time Limit in Iran Attack Decision" (translated from Hebrew), *israelspy.com*, August 10, 2012.

[26] Yaakov Katz and Yoaz Hendel, *Israel vs. Iran: The Shadow War*, Washington, DC: Potomac Books, 2012, pp. 167-193.

[27] For general background information, see "Potential Factors in an Israeli Decision: Possible Operational Aspects of an Israeli Strike" and "Potential Factors in an Israeli Decision: Estimated Effects of a Possible Strike" below.

[28] Anthony H. Cordesman and Abdullah Toukan, *Analyzing the Impact of Preventive Strikes Against Iran's Nuclear Facilities*, Center for Strategic and International Studies, September 10, 2012.

commentators have presented what they claim to be leaked information from U.S. or Israeli sources pertaining to possible operational details of potential Israeli military action.[29]

In response to a question in an August *Ha'aretz* interview about whether the potential domestic, regional, and international costs of Israeli military action would be worth "a two-year delay in Iran's inevitable nuclearization," an Israeli "decisionmaker" widely assumed to be Defense Minister Barak[30] said:

> Our objective is not to wipe out the Iranian nuclear program. But it must be understood that the real story is the contest between Iran's nuclearization and the fall of the current regime of the ayatollahs in Iran. If we succeed in pushing off the nuclear program by six or eight or 10 years, there's a good chance that the regime will not survive until the critical moment. So the objective is delay.[31]

Meir Dagan, who ended his eight-year tenure as head of Israel's Mossad in early 2011, is one of the most outspoken opponents of an Israeli strike against Iranian nuclear facilities in the near future. When interviewed for a September *New Yorker* article, Dagan said:

> An Israeli bombing would lead to a regional war and solve the internal problems of the Islamic Republic of Iran. It would galvanize Iranian society behind the leadership and create unity around the nuclear issue. And it would justify Iran in rebuilding its nuclear project and saying, 'Look, see, we were attacked by the Zionist enemy and we clearly need to have it.'[32]

U.S. Concerns and Possible Responses: Possible Impact on Israeli Decisionmaking

As mentioned above and discussed further below (see "The United States"), U.S. concerns and potential responses regarding the consequences of a possible Israeli strike on Iranian nuclear facilities could significantly affect Israeli decisionmaking. Israeli differences with the Obama Administration over the Iranian nuclear issue have reportedly been the subject of intense private discussions.[33] Additionally, U.S. concerns about regional and international perceptions of U.S. involvement in a potential Israeli attack and the durability of the international sanctions regime

---

[29] For example, in August, a U.S. blogger posted what he claimed was an Israeli briefing document outlining Israel's war plans against Iran. He claimed that the document was passed to him "by a high-level Israeli source who received it from an IDF officer. Richard Silverstein, "Bibi's Secret War Plan," *Tikun Olam*, August 15, 2012. Passages posted from the alleged document anticipate massive Israeli cyberattacks, followed by land- and naval-based missile attacks and attacks by the Israel Air Force against a wide range of Iranian nuclear facilities, military targets, and key individual professionals and commanders. Ibid. A late September report cited unnamed U.S. military and intelligence officials discussing various Israeli attack options. Mark Perry, "The Entebbe Option," *foreignpolicy.com*, September 27, 2012. A late March report by the same author also cited unnamed U.S. government officials in speculating that Israel could possibly use airfields in Azerbaijan to land planes or conduct search-and-rescue missions following an attack in Iran. Mark Perry, "Israel's Secret Staging Ground," *foreignpolicy.com*, March 28, 2012. Israeli Foreign Minister Avigdor Lieberman subsequently dismissed reports of possible Israeli use of Azeri airfields as "science fiction." Lada Evgrashina and Margarita Antidze, "Israel denies it has access to Azerbaijan air bases," *Reuters*, April 23, 2012. A late September report focused on possible Israeli

[30] Harriet Sherwood, "Israeli speculation over Iran strike reaches fever pitch," *guardian.co.uk*, August 14, 2012.

[31] Ari Shavit, "A grave warning on Iran from 'the decision maker,'" *Ha'aretz*, August 11, 2012.

[32] Remnick, op. cit.

[33] Anne Gearan, "Rep. Mike Rogers tells of heated exchange between Netanyahu, U.S. envoy over Iran nuclear program," *washingtonpost.com*, September 6, 2012.

---

against Iran may have at least partly motivated the following August 2012 comments by General Martin Dempsey, Chairman of the Joint Chiefs of Staff: "I don't want to be accused of trying to influence—nor do I want—nor do I want to be complicit if [the Israelis] choose to do it."[34]

President Obama, in his September 25 address at the annual opening session of the U.N. General Assembly in New York, said that time remains for diplomacy with Iran, but is "not unlimited."[35] He also said that the United States "will do what we must to prevent Iran from obtaining a nuclear weapon."[36] Earlier in September, the Administration apparently rejected Israeli requests both for setting firm deadlines for U.S. military action, and for an Obama-Netanyahu meeting later in the month on the sidelines of the annual opening sessions of the U.N. General Assembly.[37] In declining to set deadlines, Secretary of State Clinton set forth her view of U.S.-Israel differences on the issue in a September 2012 interview:

> They're more anxious about a quick response because they feel that they're right in the bull's-eye, so to speak. But we're convinced that we have more time to focus on these sanctions, to do everything we can to bring Iran to a good-faith negotiation.[38]

Responding at a news conference, Netanyahu was quoted as saying:

> If Iran knows that there's no deadline, what will it do? Exactly what it's doing: It's continuing without any interference toward obtaining nuclear weapons capability and from there nuclear bombs. The world tells Israel: Wait. There's still time. And I say: Wait for what? Wait until when? Those in the international community who refuse to put red lines before Iran don't have a moral right to place a red light before Israel.[39]

U.S. responses to Netanyahu's statement, including by Members of Congress, have varied.[40]

---

[34] Transcript of remarks by General Martin E. Dempsey, U.S. Embassy in London, England, August 30, 2012, available at http://www.jcs mil/speech.aspx?id=1727.

[35] Matt Spetalnick and Mark Felsenthal, "U.S. will 'do what we must' on Iran, Ban Ki-moon opposes threats," *Reuters*, September 25, 2012.

[36] Ibid.

[37] Netanyahu has subsequently consulted with President Obama via telephone, and ultimately met in New York on September 27 with Secretary of State Clinton.

[38] Indira A.R. Lakshmanan, "U.S. 'Not Setting Deadlines' for Iran, Clinton Says," *Bloomberg*, September 10, 2012.

[39] Joshua Mitnick and Jay Solomon, "Israel Blasts U.S. Over Iran—Netanyahu Says Obama Administration Has No 'Moral Right' to Restrain Jewish State," *Wall Street Journal*, September 12, 2012. An Israeli "decisionmaker" widely believed to be Defense Minister Barak was quoted as saying in August, "But let me remind you that Ronald Reagan did not want to see a nuclear Pakistan but Pakistan did go nuclear. Bill Clinton did not want to see a nuclear North Korea, but North Korea went nuclear." Shavit, "A grave warning on Iran from 'the decision maker,'" op. cit. In September, however, Barak acknowledged "impressive preparations by the Americans to counter Iran on all fronts" and asserted that some U.S. red lines for military action already existed. Barak Ravid, "Barak hints U.S. military preparations may eliminate Israel's need for Iran strike," *haaretz.com*, September 7, 2012; Golan and Korin-Lieber, op. cit.

[40] Senator Barbara Boxer, the sponsor of the U.S.-Israel Enhanced Security Cooperation Act of 2012 (P.L. 112-150), wrote a letter dated September 12 to Netanyahu urging Netanyahu to "step back and clarify your remarks so that the world sees that there is no daylight between the United States and Israel." Text available at http://boxer.senate.gov/en/press/releases/091212b.cfm. A group of 128 Republican Members of Congress sent a September 13 letter to President Obama calling on him to meet with Netanyahu during his planned U.S. visit later in the month. Text available at http://kingston house.gov/news/documentsingle.aspx?DocumentID=308403. In September 20 testimony before the Middle East and South Asia Subcommittee of the House Committee on Foreign Affairs, former deputy national security advisor (during the George W. Bush Administration) Elliott Abrams said that no president of the United States would give Israel a pledge to attack another country "by a date certain."

Regarding levels of U.S.-Israel security cooperation focused on this issue, former Obama White House national security official Dennis Ross suggested in August that "senior American officials should ask Israeli leaders if there are military capabilities we could provide them with—like additional bunker-busting bombs, tankers for refueling aircraft and targeting information—that would extend the clock for them."[41] A U.S. source has reported that the United States has drastically reduced the scope of its planned involvement in a late October joint missile defense exercise with Israel known as *Austere Challenge 12*.[42] The United States and more than 30 other countries reportedly conducted joint military maneuvers in the Persian Gulf in late September, possibly in preparation for potential Iranian responses to an Israeli attack.[43]

Potential Iranian Responses: Possible Impact on Israeli Decisionmaking

As discussed below (see "Potential Factors in an Israeli Decision: Possible Iranian Responses to a Strike"), Israeli leaders' calculations regarding Iran's potential response to an attack on its nuclear facilities may affect their decisionmaking. Leading Iranian military commanders and advisors, as well as Hezbollah's leader Hassan Nasrallah, have indicated that Iran and Hezbollah would retaliate robustly against Israel, and that Iran would possibly also target U.S. positions in the Gulf.[44] Reports indicate that Iran test-fired four surface-to-sea missiles near the Strait of Hormuz in late September, and that it is planning to hold major military preparedness maneuvers in the near future.[45] One senior Iranian Revolutionary Guard Corps (IRGC) commander reportedly said in September that Iran could launch a preemptive strike against Israel if it were sure Israel was preparing to attack it.[46] Reports from September that Iran bears responsibility for recent cyberattacks against various U.S. banks and companies[47] could presage similar attacks in retaliation for a possible Israeli military strike.

Iranian or Iranian-allied terrorist plots against Israeli targets (see "Attacks Against Israeli Interests Abroad" below) also appear to remain a threat. Several reports alleged Hezbollah involvement[48] in the July 2012 bus suicide bombing in Burgas, Bulgaria that targeted an Israeli tourist group—

---

[41] Dennis B. Ross, "How America Can Slow Israel's March to War," *New York Times*, August 17, 2012.

[42] Karl Vick and Aaron J. Klein, "Exclusive: U.S. Scales Back Military Exercise with Israel, Affecting Potential Iran Strike," *time.com*, August 31, 2012.

[43] Peter Kenyon, "U.S. Naval Exercises Send Message in the Tense Gulf," *National Public Radio*, September 24, 2012. Known as the International Mine Countermeasures Exercise (IMCMEX), the maneuvers reportedly included, among other countries, the United Kingdom, France, Japan, Yemen, and Jordan. Laura Sukhtian, "Massive Anti-Mine Naval Exercise Underway in Gulf," *Defense News*, September 17, 2012.

[44] "IRGC Commander Warns of Iran's Devastating Response to Israeli Attack," *Fars News Agency*, September 17, 2012; Laila Bassam, "Iran could strike US bases if Israel attacks: Hezbollah," *Reuters*, September 3, 2012; Zahra Hosseinian, "Iran: Hezbollah will defend us 'easily' against Israeli attack – Iran," *Reuters*, September 14, 2012.

[45] Nick Schifrin and Matthew McGarry, "Iran, US Flex Military Muscles in Persian Gulf," *ABC News*, September 25, 2012; Robert Tait, "Iran plans military exercises in preparation for Israeli strike on nuclear facilities," *telegraph.co.uk*, September 16, 2012.

[46] Zahra Hosseinian and Rania El Gamal, "Iran could launch pre-emptive Israel strike-commander," *Reuters*, September 23, 2012.

[47] Ellen Nakashima, "Iran blamed for cyberattacks on U.S. banks and companies," *Washington Post*, September 21, 2012.

[48] Nicholas Kulish and Eric Schmitt, "Hezbollah Is Blamed for Attack on Israeli Tourists in Bulgaria," *New York Times*, July 19, 2012.

---

killing six (including the Bulgarian driver) and injuring at least 32. The broader strategic purpose of such plots—i.e., whether they seek to deter or provoke possible Israeli or international action of a specific nature—is difficult to discern.

Congressional Action

In addition to enacting additional sanctions (as discussed above) against Iran in August 2012, Congress has taken other actions in 2012 with possible relevance to the Iranian nuclear issue. Congress and the President may have at least partly focused on bolstering Israeli capabilities vis-à-vis Iran in enacting the U.S.-Israel Enhanced Security Cooperation Act of 2012 (P.L. 112-150) on July 27. The Act contains non-binding "sense of Congress" language focusing largely on possible avenues of cooperation outside of direct bilateral aid, including expediting specific types of arms sales (such as F-35 fighter aircraft, refueling tankers, and bunker buster munitions); providing excess defense articles; boosting operational, intelligence, and political-military coordination; and providing additional aid for Israel's Iron Dome short-range missile defense system and U.S.-Israel cooperative missile defense programs. The Act also extended deadlines for Israel to access U.S. war reserves stockpiles and to draw upon existing loan guarantees.

Furthermore, the House passed a measure on May 27, 2012—the National Defense Authorization Act for FY2013 (H.R. 4310)—that would, if ultimately enacted, authorize up to $680 million in additional funding for Iron Dome from FY2012 to FY2015.[49] Congress and the President made an initial $205 million appropriation for the program in FY2011. An additional $70 million in U.S. funding was reprogrammed for Iron Dome in FY2012 from prior-year Missile Defense Agency funding for various programs, and will presumably count toward the $680 million figure if H.R. 4310 is enacted. Israel has reportedly spent more than $200 million on initial stages of Iron Dome's development, procurement, and deployment.[50] One report indicates that the House Armed Services Committee may seek to condition additional U.S. funding for Iron Dome on co-production or technology sharing because of the system's possible application for forward-deployed U.S. military units.[51]

On September 22, the Senate passed S.J.Res. 41 by a vote of 90-1. If subsequently passed by the House, this joint resolution would express the non-binding "sense of Congress" rejecting "any United States policy that would rely on efforts to contain a nuclear weapons-capable Iran", and joining "the President in ruling out any policy that would rely on containment as an option in response to the Iranian nuclear threat." S.J.Res. 41 explicitly states, however, that it shall not be construed as "an authorization for the use of force or a declaration of war."

The remainder of this report is unchanged from the version published on March 28, 2012.

---

[49] The version of the Department of Defense Appropriations Act, 2013 (H.R. 5856) reported by the Senate Appropriations Committee would, if enacted, provide $211 million to Israel for Iron Dome in FY2013, subject to possible budget sequestration. For information on sequestration, see CRS Report RL33222, *U.S. Foreign Aid to Israel*, by Jeremy M. Sharp

[50] Jamie Levin, "Israel's economy will pay heavy price for Iron Dome," *Ha'aretz*, March 23, 2012.

[51] Spencer Ackerman, "U.S. Funds Israel's 'Iron Dome,' But Doesn't (Quite) Know How It Works," *wired.com*, August 21, 2012.

Introduction, Issue Overview, and Questions for Congress[52]

In February 2012, a U.S. newspaper columnist reported that Secretary of Defense Leon Panetta "believes there is a strong likelihood that Israel will strike Iran in April, May or June."[53] Less than two weeks later in testimony before the Senate Armed Services Committee on February 14, Secretary Panetta declined when questioned to take a position on the likelihood of a spring 2012 Israeli attack against nuclear facilities in Iran.[54]

Secretary Panetta's comments were only part of the stream of statements from U.S. and Israeli officials and media reports that drew attention to a question that has periodically recurred in the national security discourse of both countries (and more broadly): Might Israel choose to attack Iran's nuclear facilities, possibly counter to U.S. advice?

For decades, successive regimes in Iran have engaged in nuclear-related activities. The ultimate goal of these activities, however, has remained stubbornly ambiguous. Despite extensive examination of these activities by both government and non-government experts around the world, including on-site investigation by representatives of the International Atomic Energy Agency (IAEA), no definitive proof has been offered to conclude with certainty the validity of

- Iran's claims that its nuclear work is entirely for peaceful purposes as allowed under the Nuclear Non-Proliferation Treaty (NPT) to which it is a party;

- concerns of some government officials and non-government experts in the United States and elsewhere that Iran is seeking a "nuclear capability" below the threshold of nuclear weapons (which entails the combination of fissile material with a nuclear warhead and an appropriate delivery vehicle) that nevertheless may allow it to rapidly cross the nuclear threshold at some time in the future; or

- allegations that the Iranian regime is committed to acquiring nuclear weapons.

Ongoing disagreements among analysts as to how far away Iran is from achieving a "nuclear capability" or nuclear weapons if it is committed to doing so only exacerbate this ambiguity and uncertainty regarding Iran's nuclear-related efforts. This ambiguity and uncertainty is a major feature of the environment in which international actors decide their policies and actions vis-à-vis

---

[52] Prepared by Jim Zanotti, Specialist in Middle Eastern Affairs, with contributions from Kenneth Katzman, Specialist in Middle Eastern Affairs and Paul K. Kerr, Analyst in Nonproliferation. See also CRS Report RL32048, *Iran: U.S. Concerns and Policy Responses*, by Kenneth Katzman; CRS Report RL33476, *Israel: Background and U.S. Relations*, by Jim Zanotti; and CRS Report R40094, *Iran's Nuclear Program: Tehran's Compliance with International Obligations*, by Paul K. Kerr. Outside reports on the issue include Anthony H. Cordesman and Alexander Wilner, *Iran and the Gulf Military Balance – II: The Missile and Nuclear Dimensions: Working Draft*, Center for Strategic and International Studies, February 22, 2012. Ronen Bergman, "Will Israel Attack Iran?", *New York Times Magazine*, January 25, 2012; Dalia Dassa Kaye, et al., *Israel and Iran: A Dangerous Rivalry*, RAND Corporation, 2011; Dana H. Allin and Steven Simon, *The Sixth Crisis: Iran, Israel, America and the Rumors of War*, New York: Oxford University Press, 2010.

[53] David Ignatius, "Of a mind to attack Iran," *Washington Post*, February 3, 2012.

[54] At the same hearing, Secretary Panetta acknowledged having talked with the columnist who wrote the February 2012 report "about a lot of things."

Iran. The view a state holds of the ultimate goal of Iran's nuclear-related activities informs the approach it takes in dealing with the Iranian regime.

For various reasons—including geopolitical, historical, and ideological—the prospect of an Iran with nuclear weapons arguably affects the threat perceptions of Israel more than those of the United States[55] or other nations. Twice in its history, Israel has conducted air strikes aimed at preventing a regional actor from acquiring a nuclear weapons capability—destroying Iraq's Tammuz-Osirak reactor in 1981 and a presumed reactor under construction at Al Kibar near Deir al Zur in Syria in 2007. For some period of time, Israeli leaders have conveyed their view that Israel may similarly be compelled to act to prevent a potentially nuclear-armed Iran. Analysts generally agree that Israeli military action against multiple Iranian nuclear facilities would be significantly more complex operationally than these previous attacks, both of which targeted single facilities that were closer in range to Israel (see **Figure 1** below). What lessons the previous strikes—particularly the one on Osirak in 1981—impart for an Israeli decision on whether to strike Iran is a subject of debate.[56]

For Congress, the potential impact—short- and long-term—of an Israeli decision regarding Iran and its implementation is a critical issue of concern.

Since Iran's nuclear program became a major international issue a decade ago, Israel has deferred to the United States and other actors in coordinating diplomacy and implementing economic and other sanctions aimed at convincing Iran to abandon activities that could allow it to develop nuclear weapons. In recent years, however, reports suggest that Israel has pursued covert means—including sabotage, cyberwarfare, and assassination—to intimidate Iran and delay the nuclear program, with some reported success.[57] Without confirming or denying involvement, Israeli officials also generally have welcomed reports of events that might set back Iran's nuclear program.[58]

Even before the reports in recent months of possible Israeli military action, at various stages of the international effort to persuade Iran to relinquish any possible nuclear weapons ambitions some Israeli officials have hinted that Israel might be compelled to take unilateral action to counter what they see as an Iranian nuclear weapons program.[59] It was in the first three months of

---

[55] Leslie Susser, "Spy vs. Spy," *Jerusalem Report*, March 26, 2012, stating, "Although he too is committed to stopping the Iranians, US President Barack Obama does not see the prospect of a nuclear Iran in the same apocalyptic terms as Netanyahu does. True, a nuclear Iran would hurt vital American interests in the Middle East, but Iran is a long way from American shores."

[56] Allin and Simon, p. 53. Some analysts cite Osirak to emphasize the potential perils of an attack on Iran, pointing to Saddam Hussein's subsequent clandestine pursuit of nuclear weapons on an accelerated timetable. Some use it to emphasize the potential benefits of an attack, pointing to the U.S.-led international action from 1991-2003 that eventually squelched Hussein's nuclear ambitions, even though the international coalition was not initially assembled in response to Iraq's nuclear program, but its 1990 invasion of Kuwait. According to a 2010 book, many Israelis believe that buying time through a strike on Iran "might prove worthwhile in [unanticipated] ways..." Ibid.

[57] See Yossi Melman, "The war against Iran's nuclear program has already begun," *Ha'aretz*, December 2, 2011. Some reports state that U.S. and British intelligence agencies have aided Israel with some non-lethal covert operations. Daniel Klaidman, Eli Lake, and Dan Ephron, "Obama's Dangerous Game with Iran," *Newsweek*, February 13, 2012.

[58] For example, after the January 2012 assassination of an Iranian nuclear scientist, Brig. Gen. Yoav Mordechai, an Israeli military spokesman, reportedly wrote on his Facebook page, "I don't know who took revenge on the Iranian scientist, but I am definitely not shedding a tear." Alan Cowell and Rick Gladstone, "Iran Reports Killing of Nuclear Scientist in 'Terrorist' Blast," *New York Times*, January 11, 2012.

[59] See, e.g., Jeffrey Goldberg, "Point of No Return," *The Atlantic*, September 2010.

2012, however, that the issue came into sharper relief for U.S. policymakers, including in Congress. This was in part a result of comments by senior Israeli government officials and former officials that intensified the debate within their country as to the wisdom and potential effectiveness of military action against nuclear-related targets in Iran, linked to a similar discussion in the United States and worldwide.

This report assesses this issue, focusing primarily on the decision that might be made by the government of Israel. In particular, it examines the range of factors that could influence such an Israeli decision.

Implementation of an Israeli decision to strike Iran's nuclear-related facilities could have significant implications for U.S. interests and goals related both to the nuclear issue itself and to broader regional and international concerns, including U.S. relations with Israel.[60] In assessing those implications and considering possible action either before or after a possible Israeli strike (see "Conclusion: Possible Implications for Congress" below), Congress and the Obama Administration might consider the following questions:

Israeli Debate and Decision Regarding a Potential Attack:

- What is the nature of the public and official debate in Israel over the Iranian nuclear issue and possible Israeli, U.S., and international approaches to it, including military and non-military options? How might that debate evolve?

- What are the factors in Israeli thinking and who are the main actors involved in the decision?

- Under what conditions is a final political decision regarding military action likely?

- How does Israel assess the operational requirements of a potential strike?

Effect on Iran's Nuclear Program and Regime:

- Ultimately, is an attack more likely to prevent an Iran with nuclear weapons or help bring it about? If an attack only delayed a potential nuclear weapons program in Iran, would Israel feel compelled to take additional military action later?

- What effect might an attack have on a potential Iranian decision to weaponize its nuclear program?

- Would an attack help or hinder the ongoing international effort to use diplomacy, monitoring, sanctions, and possible threats of further military action to persuade Iran not to pursue nuclear weapons? To what extent might the large coalition that is now working with the United States to enforce sanctions against Iran fracture in the event of a strike?

- Would an attack strengthen or weaken the Iranian regime, particularly given that current trends indicate that the regime faces significant economic challenges and political divisions?

---

[60] For more information on U.S.-Israel relations, including the level of U.S. commitment to Israel's security, see CRS Report RL33476, *Israel: Background and U.S. Relations*, by Jim Zanotti; and CRS Report RL33222, *U.S. Foreign Aid to Israel*, by Jeremy M. Sharp.

Effect on Other U.S. Interests:

- What retaliation from Iran and its regional allies (including Lebanese Hezbollah and Hamas or other Palestinian militants) is likely against Israeli targets?

- If Iran retaliated, would it limit the targeted area to Israel, or would it also target U.S. interests and allies in the region and elsewhere? If Iran expands its response to U.S. or U.S.-allied targets, what forms might that take?

- What is the likelihood and potential scope of a crisis in the Strait of Hormuz and Persian Gulf regarding global energy prices and potential region-wide conflict? What are other possible regional consequences of an Israeli attack?

This report has many elements that are the subject of vigorous debate and remain fully or partially outside public knowledge. CRS does not claim that it has confirmed independently any sources cited within this report that attribute specific positions or views to Israeli, U.S., or other officials.

Iran's Nuclear Program and Facilities of Main Concern: A Primer[61]

Iran's leaders claim that Iran's nuclear program is solely for peaceful, civilian energy and research purposes. Since the 1979 Islamic Revolution, Iran's leaders (including current Supreme Leader Ayatollah Ali Khamene'i) have regularly spoken in public against the development and use of nuclear weapons.[62] Iran is a party to the Nuclear Non-Proliferation Treaty (NPT) and conducts its declared nuclear activities under International Atomic Energy Agency (IAEA) monitoring and safeguards. For a discussion of Iran's compliance or non-compliance with international obligations regarding its nuclear program, see **Figure 2** below and CRS Report R40094, *Iran's Nuclear Program: Tehran's Compliance with International Obligations*, by Paul K. Kerr.

Iran's gas centrifuge-based uranium enrichment program is currently the main source of proliferation concern for the international community. Gas centrifuges enrich uranium by spinning uranium hexafluoride gas at high speeds to increase the concentration of the uranium-235 isotope. Such centrifuges can produce both low-enriched uranium (LEU), which can be used in nuclear power reactors, and highly enriched uranium (HEU).[63] HEU and plutonium are the two types of fissile material used in nuclear weapons.

Iran's construction of a nuclear reactor moderated by heavy water has also been a source of proliferation concern. The reactor is a proliferation concern because the reactor's spent fuel will contain plutonium well-suited for use in nuclear weapons. To be used in nuclear weapons, however, plutonium must be separated from the spent fuel—a procedure called "reprocessing." Iran has said that it will not engage in reprocessing, and there is no public evidence that Tehran either has constructed or is constructing a reprocessing facility.

A 2007 National Intelligence Estimate said that Iran "probably would use covert facilities—rather than its declared nuclear sites—for the production of highly enriched uranium for a weapon,"[64] at least in part because of the difficulty of diverting significant amounts of nuclear material from safeguarded facilities without detection. According to Colin Kahl, Deputy Assistant Secretary of Defense for Middle East Policy from 2009 until the end of 2011, "there is no evidence that Iran has built additional covert enrichment plants."[65]

For a January 31, 2012, Senate Select Intelligence Committee hearing, James Clapper, Director of National Intelligence, submitted written testimony stating that Iran has the "capacity to eventually produce nuclear weapons" and "is keeping open the option to develop" such weapons, but added that "[w]e do not know... if Iran will eventually decide to build nuclear weapons."

Some high-ranking U.S. and Israeli political decisionmakers reportedly differ on the question of how long action might remain possible to prevent a potentially nuclear-armed Iran. This relates to the question of a possible "zone of immunity" discussed below. Differences on this question reportedly persist even though U.S. and Israeli assessments are similar on the timetables for Iran to

- achieve the capability to develop and produce the components for a nuclear weapon; and

- if it chooses, to weaponize successfully.

In a January 2012 *60 Minutes* interview, Secretary of Defense Leon Panetta said, "The consensus is that, if [Iran] decided to do it, it would probably take them about a year to be able to produce a bomb and then possibly another one to two years in order to put it on a deliverable vehicle of some sort in order to deliver that weapon."[66]

According a February 2012 report from IAEA Director-General Yukiya Amano, Iran has produced 5,451 kilograms of LEU in the

---

[61] Prepared by Paul K. Kerr, Analyst in Nonproliferation, with contributions from Jim Zanotti, Specialist in Middle Eastern Affairs.

[62] President Obama was quoted in a late February 2012 interview as saying that Iranian leaders in early 2012 have been saying that "nuclear weapons are sinful and un-Islamic." President Barack Obama, quoted in Jeffrey Goldberg, "Obama to Iran and Israel: 'As President of the United States, I Don't Bluff,'" *theatlantic.com*, March 2, 2012.

[63] LEU typically contains less than 5% uranium-235. Weapons-grade HEU typically contains approximately 90% uranium-235.

[64] Similarly, a CIA report for 2004 concluded that "inspections and safeguards will most likely prevent Tehran from using facilities declared to the IAEA directly for its weapons program as long as Iran remains a party to the NPT." *Unclassified Report to Congress on the Acquisition of Technology Relating to Weapons of Mass Destruction and Advanced Conventional Munitions*, January 1-December 31, 2004.

[65] Colin H. Kahl, "Not Time to Attack Iran: Why War Should be a Last Resort," *Foreign Affairs*, January 17, 2012.

[66] Transcript of remarks by Secretary Panetta from CBS's *60 Minutes* interview, January 29, 2012, available at http://www.votesmart.org/public-statement/664274/cbs-60-minutes-transcript.

Natanz commercial facility. This quantity of LEU, if further enriched, could produce enough HEU for four nuclear weapons, according to the Institute for Science and International Security.[67] According to Amano's report, Iran has enriched approximately 95 kilograms of uranium up to 20% uranium-235 at the Natanz pilot facility and approximately 14 kilograms of similarly enriched uranium at the Fordow facility.

The four facilities described below are under IAEA safeguards and monitoring:

Natanz

Iran has both a pilot centrifuge facility and a larger commercial facility located at this site. The commercial facility is reportedly hardened by steel-reinforced concrete, buried underground, and covered by a mound of earth.[68] This facility is capable of eventually holding more than 47,000 centrifuges. Iran is currently using first-generation centrifuges in the commercial facility to produce uranium enriched up to 5% uranium-235. Iran is using the pilot facility both to produce uranium enriched up to 20% uranium-235 and also to test more-advanced centrifuges. According to the IAEA Director-General's February 2012 report, Iran has installed approximately 9,100 centrifuges in the commercial facility and is feeding uranium hexafluoride into as many as 8,808 of those centrifuges.

Fordow

Iran has a centrifuge facility located at this site—reportedly built into the side of a small mountain[69] and specially hardened.[70] The facility is eventually supposed to contain approximately 3,000 centrifuges. Tehran has told the IAEA that the facility will be configured to produce both uranium enriched to 5% uranium-235 and 20% uranium-235. Iran has installed approximately 700 first-generation centrifuges in the facility, and it is now reportedly producing 20%-enriched uranium.

Esfahan

Among several nuclear facilities located at this site, Iran's above-ground uranium conversion facility converts uranium oxide into several compounds, including gaseous uranium hexafluoride that can be enriched in centrifuges.

Arak

Iran is constructing a nuclear reactor moderated by heavy water at this above-ground site. Tehran also has a plant at this site for producing heavy water. According to a February 2012 IAEA report, the plant appears to be operating.

Iran also has other nuclear-related facilities, including a light-water nuclear power reactor at Bushehr and a research reactor in Tehran, as well as research, centrifuge production, and mining facilities. See "Effect on Iran's Nuclear Program" below for a textbox describing other facilities related to Iran's nuclear program.

Figure 1 below provides a map showing facilities related or possibly related to Iran's nuclear program, the site of the two previous Israeli strikes in Iraq and Syria, and the surrounding region. **Figure 2** below provides a timeline of selected events relevant to the Iranian nuclear issue and Israel's involvement.

(...continued)

[67] *ISIS Analysis of IAEA Iran Safeguards Report: Production of 20% Enriched Uranium Triples; Iran Increases Number of Enriching Centrifuges at Natanz FEP by Nearly 50% and Signals an Intention to Greatly Expand the Number of Centrifuges at Both Natanz and Fordow; Advanced Centrifuge Program Appears Troubled*, Institute for Science and International Security, February 24, 2012.

[68] Todd Lindeman and Bill Webster, "Hardened targets," *Washington Post*, March 1, 2012.

[69] Ibid.

[70] Joby Warrick, "Iran: Underground sites vulnerable, experts say," *Washington Post*, March 1, 2012.

Figure 1. Map of Major Iranian Facilities in Regional Context

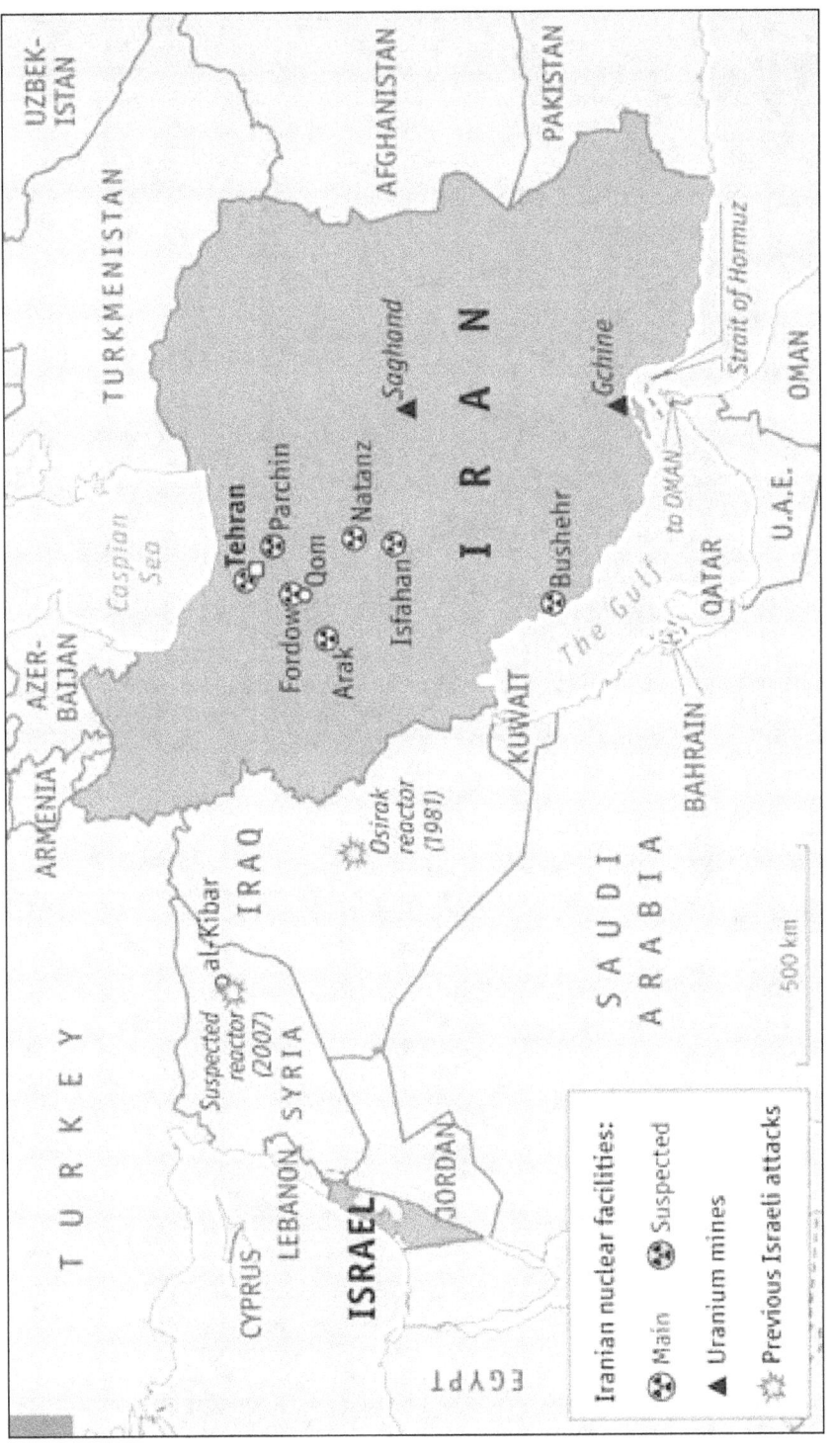

Sources: *Economist*, adapted by CRS.

Notes: All locations are approximate. Parchin is an Iranian military testing facility that, according to the *Washington Post*, "U.S. officials believe was used a decade ago to test explosive triggers of the kind used to detonate nuclear warheads." Thomas Erdbrink and Joby Warrick, "Iran urged to grant access to inspectors," *Washington Post*, March 9, 2012. According to the IAEA Director-General's November 2011 report, the IAEA was "permitted by Iran to visit the site twice in 2005. From satellite imagery available at that time, the Agency identified a number of areas of interest, none of which, however, included the location now believed to contain the building which houses the explosives chamber mentioned above; consequently, the Agency's visits did not uncover anything of relevance." In early March 2012, the "P5+1" countries (United States, United Kingdom, France, Germany, China, Russia) that manage international diplomacy with Iran on the nuclear issue urged Iran to grant IAEA monitors renewed access to Parchin. See **Figure 3** for additional reported details on the underground facilities at Natanz and Fordow.

Figure 2. Timeline of Relevant Events Involving Iran's Nuclear Program and Israel
2002-2012

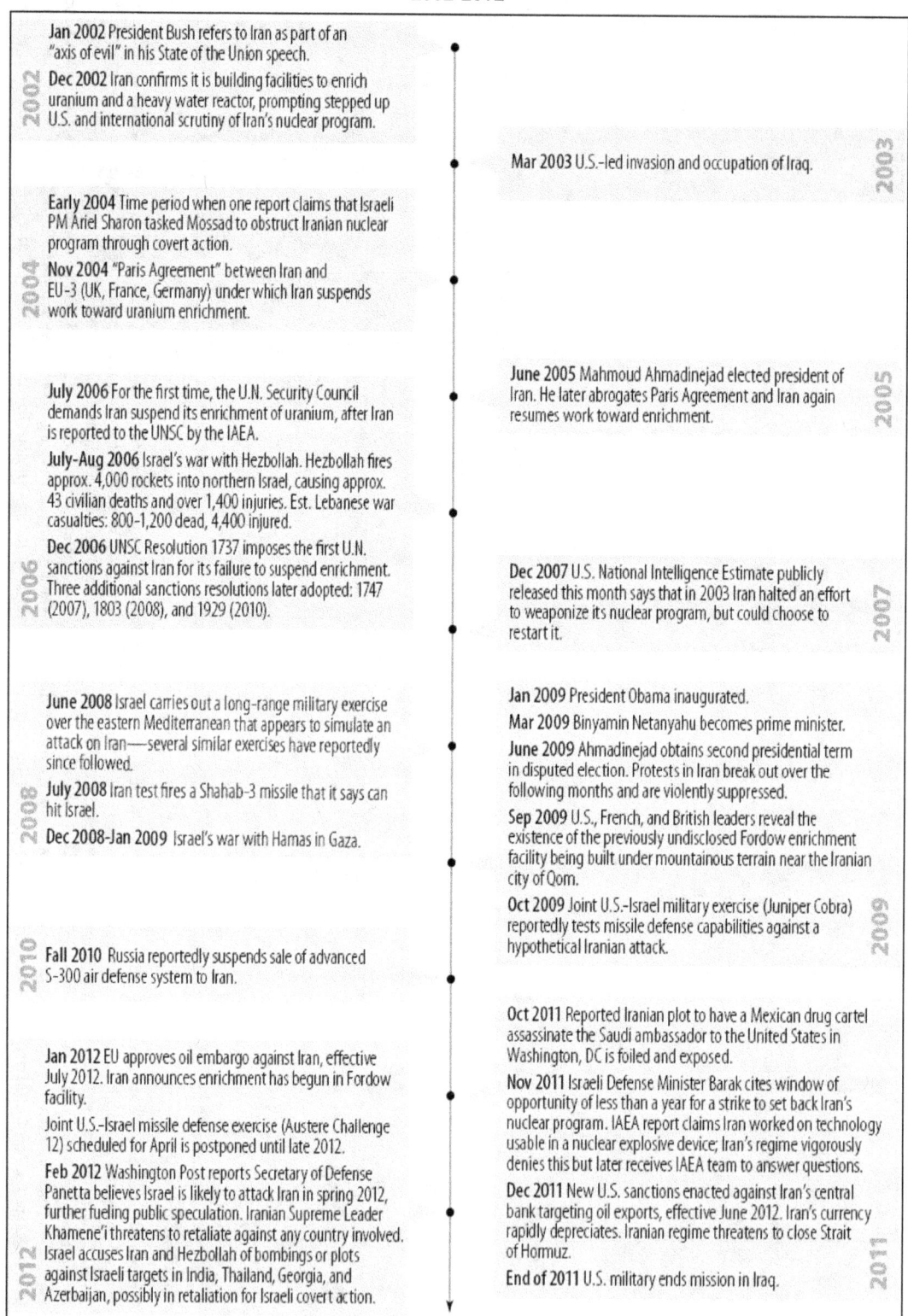

Jan 2002 President Bush refers to Iran as part of an "axis of evil" in his State of the Union speech.

Dec 2002 Iran confirms it is building facilities to enrich uranium and a heavy water reactor, prompting stepped up U.S. and international scrutiny of Iran's nuclear program.

Mar 2003 U.S.-led invasion and occupation of Iraq.

Early 2004 Time period when one report claims that Israeli PM Ariel Sharon tasked Mossad to obstruct Iranian nuclear program through covert action.

Nov 2004 "Paris Agreement" between Iran and EU-3 (UK, France, Germany) under which Iran suspends work toward uranium enrichment.

June 2005 Mahmoud Ahmadinejad elected president of Iran. He later abrogates Paris Agreement and Iran again resumes work toward enrichment.

July 2006 For the first time, the U.N. Security Council demands Iran suspend its enrichment of uranium, after Iran is reported to the UNSC by the IAEA.

July-Aug 2006 Israel's war with Hezbollah. Hezbollah fires approx. 4,000 rockets into northern Israel, causing approx. 43 civilian deaths and over 1,400 injuries. Est. Lebanese war casualties: 800-1,200 dead, 4,400 injured.

Dec 2006 UNSC Resolution 1737 imposes the first U.N. sanctions against Iran for its failure to suspend enrichment. Three additional sanctions resolutions later adopted: 1747 (2007), 1803 (2008), and 1929 (2010).

Dec 2007 U.S. National Intelligence Estimate publicly released this month says that in 2003 Iran halted an effort to weaponize its nuclear program, but could choose to restart it.

June 2008 Israel carries out a long-range military exercise over the eastern Mediterranean that appears to simulate an attack on Iran—several similar exercises have reportedly since followed.

July 2008 Iran test fires a Shahab-3 missile that it says can hit Israel.

Dec 2008-Jan 2009 Israel's war with Hamas in Gaza.

Jan 2009 President Obama inaugurated.

Mar 2009 Binyamin Netanyahu becomes prime minister.

June 2009 Ahmadinejad obtains second presidential term in disputed election. Protests in Iran break out over the following months and are violently suppressed.

Sep 2009 U.S., French, and British leaders reveal the existence of the previously undisclosed Fordow enrichment facility being built under mountainous terrain near the Iranian city of Qom.

Oct 2009 Joint U.S.-Israel military exercise (Juniper Cobra) reportedly tests missile defense capabilities against a hypothetical Iranian attack.

Fall 2010 Russia reportedly suspends sale of advanced S-300 air defense system to Iran.

Oct 2011 Reported Iranian plot to have a Mexican drug cartel assassinate the Saudi ambassador to the United States in Washington, DC is foiled and exposed.

Nov 2011 Israeli Defense Minister Barak cites window of opportunity of less than a year for a strike to set back Iran's nuclear program. IAEA report claims Iran worked on technology usable in a nuclear explosive device; Iran's regime vigorously denies this but later receives IAEA team to answer questions.

Jan 2012 EU approves oil embargo against Iran, effective July 2012. Iran announces enrichment has begun in Fordow facility.

Joint U.S.-Israel missile defense exercise (Austere Challenge 12) scheduled for April is postponed until late 2012.

Feb 2012 Washington Post reports Secretary of Defense Panetta believes Israel is likely to attack Iran in spring 2012, further fueling public speculation. Iranian Supreme Leader Khamene'i threatens to retaliate against any country involved. Israel accuses Iran and Hezbollah of bombings or plots against Israeli targets in India, Thailand, Georgia, and Azerbaijan, possibly in retaliation for Israeli covert action.

Dec 2011 New U.S. sanctions enacted against Iran's central bank targeting oil exports, effective June 2012. Iran's currency rapidly depreciates. Iranian regime threatens to close Strait of Hormuz.

End of 2011 U.S. military ends mission in Iraq.

Sources: Various, compiled by CRS.

Preliminary Considerations Regarding an Israeli Decision[71]

Nature of the Threat—Differing Stated Perceptions

The question of whether a nuclear-weapons-capable Iran will or will not pose an existential threat to Israel has become an important debate among Israeli leaders. Some Israeli officials express concerns, based on Iranian leaders' long-standing pronouncements against the existence of Israel,[72] that Iran might seek to use a nuclear weapon against Israel even if faced with the prospect of near-certain retaliation[73] from Israel's presumed but officially undeclared nuclear arsenal.[74] In a 2010 interview, Israeli Prime Minister Binyamin Netanyahu was quoted as saying:

> Iran has threatened to annihilate a state. In historical terms, this is an astounding thing. It's a monumental outrage that goes effectively unchallenged in the court of public opinion....

---

[71] Prepared by Jim Zanotti, Specialist in Middle Eastern Affairs, with contributions from Kenneth Katzman, Specialist in Middle Eastern Affairs and Paul K. Kerr, Analyst in Nonproliferation.

[72] Israeli official and public discourse regularly refers to many of these actual and alleged pronouncements. Ayatollah Ruhollah Khomeini, leader of Iran's Islamic Revolution, decreed that the elimination of a Zionist regime in Israel was a religious duty. His successor as supreme leader, Ayatollah Ali Khamene'i, has repeatedly referred to Israel as a "cancerous tumor" since his accession in 1989, including in a rare Friday sermon at a Tehran mosque in February 2012. Elected President Mahmoud Ahmadinejad quoted Khomeini when he made a remark in October 2005 that was widely translated in Israel and Western countries as expressing the hope that Israel would eventually be "wiped off the map," though some analysts have claimed that a more accurate translation was "this regime occupying Jerusalem must vanish from the page of time." Juan Cole, "Hitchens the Hacker; And, Hitchens the Orientalist; And, 'We don't Want Your Stinking War!'", *Informed Comment*, May 3, 2006. Ahmadinejad also has reportedly described the Holocaust as a "myth" used as a pretext to create an "artificial Zionist regime." In a March 2012 CNN interview, an advisor to Khamene'i said that Ahmadinejad's comments were "definitely not" meant in a military sense and that such an approach was not "a policy of Iran." "Top Iran official calls for cooperation from West in return for 'transparency,'" CNN, March 15, 2012.

[73] Ali Akbar Hashemi Rafsanjani, a former Iranian president (1989-1997), said in a December 2001 speech, "If one day, the Islamic world is also equipped with weapons like those that Israel possesses now, then the imperialists' strategy will reach a standstill because the use of even one nuclear bomb inside Israel will destroy everything. However, it will only harm the Islamic world. It is not irrational to contemplate such an eventuality." Translation by BBC Global Monitoring of Rafsanjani's Jerusalem Day speech (from Farsi) in Tehran, December 14, 2001, as carried by Voice of the Islamic Republic of Iran, available at http://www.globalsecurity.org/wmd/library/news/iran/2001/011214-text.html. However, Iranian officials, including Ahmadinejad, have made the case that Iran does not have a history of aggression. For example, in 2006, Javad Zarif, then Iran's permanent representative to the United Nations, said, "Our history, in the past 250 years, we have not attacked any other country. We have been the subject of invasion; we have been the subject of aggression; we have been the subject of use of chemical weapons. But we have defended ourselves, but we never resorted to use of chemical weapons, even in retaliation. So our record is very clear. On the other hand, unfortunately, Israel has a record of aggression against its neighbors, has a known nuclear stockpile, is not a member of any international instrument." Transcript of PBS Newshour, April 28, 2006.

[74] Israel is not a party to the NPT and maintains a policy of "nuclear opacity" or *amimut*. A consensus among media and analysts' reports is that Israel possesses an arsenal of 80 to 200 nuclear weapons, although some suggest a higher figure. See, e.g., International Institute for Strategic Studies, *Nuclear programmes in the Middle East: In the shadow of Iran*, May 2008, p. 133.

Iranian leaders talk about Israel's destruction or disappearance while simultaneously creating weapons to ensure its disappearance.[75]

Other leading Israeli officials and analysts—including Defense Minister Ehud Barak and Tamir Pardo, director of Israel's Mossad intelligence agency—generally avoid characterizing the threat from Iran as existential at least partly because they claim that Israel "is a strong state and it could protect itself under any circumstances."[76] According to three Israeli analysts, including a former deputy national security advisor, whether or not Iran will behave as a "rational actor" has "become an important dimension of the Israeli debate about a nuclear Iran."[77]

Yet, even some Israeli officials who generally avoid characterizing the threat of a nuclear-weapons-capable Iran as existential describe it as still presenting unacceptably high risks. They express concern that a nuclear Iran would compromise traditional Israeli security doctrine and practices—based on principles of self-reliance and maintaining overwhelming military superiority—and lead to an unacceptable level of national security uncertainty. This in turn would fundamentally damage the quality of life and psychological sense of safety that Israelis deem critically important to their country's continued viability as a Jewish national home.[78] According to a March 2012 article in Israel's *Jerusalem Report*, "Even if the Iranians don't use the bomb, [Netanyahu] fears the very fact that they have it could lead to a mass exodus of Jews from an Israel under nuclear threat, weakening the state and compromising the Zionist dream."[79]

Some Israelis worry that even if Iran did not attack Israel with a nuclear weapon, mere possession of a weapon or the capability to assemble one quickly would make it more difficult to deter Iran from pursuing greater regional influence and amplifying threats to Israeli security through proxies and allies—the Lebanese Shiite group Hezbollah, Hamas and other Palestinian militants in Gaza, and possibly even the beleaguered Asad regime in Syria. Some in Israel, however, argue that Iran might be limited in its ability to use a potential nuclear weapons capability to thwart conventional Israeli military action against regional threats.[80] Analysts discuss a range of other possible regional reactions that would undermine Israeli security, including less willingness of Gulf Arab states to oppose Iranian ambitions; the possibility of proliferation in countries such as Egypt, Turkey, and Saudi Arabia; and perhaps international pressure on Israel either to declare its nuclear weapons status or consider giving it up if Iran would do the same.[81]

---

[75] Goldberg, "Point of No Return," op. cit.

[76] Avner Cohen, "Israel ponders a nuclear Iran," *Bulletin of the Atomic Scientists* (Web edition), August 17, 2010. See also Barak Ravid, "Mossad chief: Nuclear Iran not necessarily existential threat to Israel," *Ha'aretz*, December 29, 2011. A February 2012 Center for Strategic and International Studies (CSIS) report stated, "In actual practice, Israel can already deliver an 'existential' nuclear strike on Iran, and will have far more capability to damage Iran than Iran is likely to have against Israel for the next decade." Cordesman and Wilner, op. cit. The *Washington Post* has written that President Obama "has declined to call on Israeli leaders to declare [its nuclear] program, a source of frustration and fear in the Middle East." Scott Wilson, "Obama to urge Israel's patience," *Washington Post*, March 3, 2012.

[77] Shai Feldman, Shlomo Brom, and Shimon Stein, "What to Do About Nuclearizing Iran? The Israeli Debate," Brandeis University, Crown Center for Middle East Studies Brief No. 59, February 2012.

[78] Haim Malka, *Crossroads: The Future of the U.S.-Israel Strategic Partnership*, Center for Strategic and International Studies, 2011, pp. 58-59; Kaye, et al., op. cit., pp. 37, 52-53.

[79] Susser, op. cit.

[80] Stein, et al., "The Public Discussion of Israel's Strategy Regarding a Nuclear Iran," op. cit.

[81] Kaye, et al., op. cit., pp. 27-28; Cohen, op. cit.; Shimon Stein, Shai Feldman, and Shlomo Brom, "The Public Discussion of Israel's Strategy Regarding a Nuclear Iran," *Institute for National Security Studies Insight* No. 310, January 31, 2012. Israel has expressed support for a WMD-free zone in the Middle East, but has asserted that other regional countries should reconcile themselves to Israel's existence before negotiating such a zone. Sha'ul Horev, (continued...)

Israelis continue to debate whether the risks of a nuclear-weapons-capable Iran outweigh the risks of a strike that most assessments doubt would definitively end Iran's nuclear program (see "Effect on Iran's Nuclear Program" below). According to one Israeli report, "Netanyahu faces one of the most difficult choices any Israeli prime minister has had to contemplate. A strike against Iran's nuclear facilities could lead to regional conflagration, tens of thousands of missiles and rockets raining down on Israeli population centers and war on several fronts. But with no attack, Iran could go nuclear on his watch."[82] Unlike the wide range of views expressed among U.S. and international analysts about whether a nuclear-weapons-capable Iran might or might not be contained, based on concepts and experiences dating from the Cold War, Israeli officials— according to a 2011 RAND Corporation report—appear to be "reluctant to address futures involving a nuclear-armed Iran, as they [want] to maintain the focus on preventing such an outcome."[83] Some Israeli analysts have, however, contemplated the prospects for mutual deterrence between Israel and Iran, including some who collaborated on the subject in a 2008 memorandum published by Israel's Institute for National Security Studies (INSS), under the assumption that Iran might not be prevented from acquiring a nuclear weapons capability. One article from this memorandum questioned whether Cold War-era containment would be applicable:

> The fact that since Hiroshima and Nagasaki no nuclear device has been used in the course of hostilities might lead to the tentative conclusion that a third use of a nuclear weapon in war is of very low probability. This conclusion is based on the superpowers relationship during the Cold War—the only historical example of a relatively stable and long nuclear deterrence balance. But would this pattern recur in various regional nuclear conflicts?[84]

Despite Israelis' general reluctance to discuss containment scenarios, some Israeli public figures are less expansive in their characterization of the inherent risks of a potentially nuclear-armed Iran. In the words of one analyst:

> If and when there was a clear Iranian threat to attack Israel, then Israel could launch a preemptive assault. And if no such threat ever materializes, Israel need never attack. Any

---

(...continued)
Director General of Israel's Atomic Energy Commission, explained the government's position in September 2009, "It is our vision and policy, to establish the Middle East as a mutually verifiable zone free of weapons of mass destruction and their delivery systems. We have always emphasized, that such a process, through direct negotiations, should begin with confidence building measures. They should be followed by mutual recognition, reconciliation, and peaceful relations. Consequently conventional and non-conventional arms control measures will emerge ... In our view, progress towards realizing this vision cannot be made without a fundamental change in regional circumstances, including a significant transformation in the attitude of states in the region towards Israel." Statement by Dr. Sha'ul Horev, Director General, Israel Atomic Energy Commission, to the 53rd General Conference of the International Atomic Energy Agency, September 2009, Israel Atomic Energy Commission, September 15, 2009.

[82] Susser, op. cit.

[83] Kaye, et al., op. cit., p. 47.

[84] Yair Evron, "An Israel-Iran Balance of Nuclear Deterrence: Seeds of Instability," *Israel and a Nuclear Iran: Implications for Arms Control, Deterrence, and Defense*, INSS Memorandum No. 94, July 2008. For an Israeli perspective on whether missile defense systems could effectively deter a "rational" Iran, see Uzi Rubin, "Missile Defense and Israel's Deterrence against a Nuclear Iran," from the same memorandum. In February 2012, Louis René Beres, a Purdue University professor with significant past involvement in assisting Israel formulate national security strategy, co-authored an essay that said, "Perhaps a nuclear Iran can still be prevented by preemption. But in the more likely absence of any remaining options for 'anticipatory self-defense,' Israel's best available stance will be to effectively deter an already-nuclear Iran." Louis René Beres and General (USAF ret.) John T. Chain, "Israel and Iran at the eleventh hour," Oxford University Press Blog, February 23, 2012.

---

future Iran-Israel war will happen if Iran's regime makes it unavoidable, not in theory but in actual practice.[85]

Possible "Zone of Immunity" and Israel's Ability to Act Independently

Long-standing Israeli national security doctrine emphasizes Israel's prerogative to "defend itself, by itself." In a January 24, 2012, speech in the Knesset, Prime Minister Netanyahu said, in reference to the Iranian nuclear issue, "In the end, with regard to threats to our very existence, we cannot abandon our future to the hands of others. With regard to our fate, our duty is to rely on ourselves alone."[86]

In a November 2011 CNN interview, Israeli Defense Minister Ehud Barak appeared to set forth parameters for Israel's ability to act independently when he said that the window of opportunity for a preventive strike to stop or slow Iran's progress toward nuclear weapons capability could close within nine months. He explained that the Iranians could enter a "zone of immunity" from military action "by widening [the] redundancy of their plan, making it spread over many more [sites], with many more elements."[87] As evidence of his claim that Iran is progressing toward a zone of immunity, Barak has cited Iran's ongoing movement of enriched uranium and/or uranium enrichment centrifuges into the supposedly difficult-to-attack Fordow facility.[88]

It is unclear whether Israeli leaders' willingness to make policy decisions in line with the zone of immunity concept explained by Barak might be affected by the views of U.S. military planners who reportedly question the imminence of Iran achieving such a zone.[89] According to a February 2012 *New York Times* article, a senior Obama Administration official who has discussed the concept with Israelis says that "'there are many other options' to slow Iran's march to a completed weapon, like shutting off Iran's oil revenues, taking out facilities that supply centrifuge parts or singling out installations where the Iranians would turn the fuel into a weapon."[90]

The concept Barak has articulated may anticipate that Iran would consider using IAEA-monitored and -safeguarded enrichment facilities at Fordow to produce weapons-grade enriched uranium. Although it is unclear how Iran may act, there is no precedent for an NPT party to use declared facilities to produce fissile material for nuclear weapons.[91] If weapons-grade enrichment were to

---

[85] Barry Rubin, "Israel Isn't Going to Attack Iran and Neither Will the United States," *PJ Media*, January 26, 2012.

[86] Transcript of English translation (from Hebrew) available on Israeli Prime Minister's Office website.

[87] Transcript of remarks by Ehud Barak on CNN's *Fareed Zakaria GPS*, November 20, 2011. According to one report, "Iran has announced plans for 10 new enrichment sites—further dispersing later-generation centrifuges in places smaller, harder to locate and easier to harden." Karl Vick, "Can Israel Stop Iran's Nuke Effort?", *Time*, February 6, 2012.

[88] "Israel and Iran: Closer to take-off," *Economist*, February 11, 2012. A report dated February 24, 2012, from IAEA Director-General Yukiya Amano said that Iran began using the site in December 2011 to enrich uranium up to 20% uranium-235. Iranian officials have stated that this uranium will be used as fuel in nuclear reactors to produce medical isotopes. "Iran Plans Several New Nuclear Reactors," PressTV, April 12, 2011.

[89] Joby Warrick, "Iran's underground nuclear sites not immune to U.S. bunker-busters, experts say," *Washington Post*, March 1, 2012.

[90] Mark Landler and David E. Sanger, "U.S. and Israel Split on Speed of Iran Threat," *New York Times*, February 8, 2012.

[91] North Korea used plutonium instead of uranium-enriching centrifuges to provide fissile material for its nuclear weapons program and announced its withdrawal from the NPT in 2003, "two years before announcing that it had the (continued...)

---

occur at Fordow or Natanz under IAEA safeguards (assuming that Iran was cooperating with the IAEA), the international community would probably learn of it because of the difficulty in diverting significant amounts of nuclear material from safeguarded centrifuge facilities without detection.[92]

To put the current Israeli debate into context, one report has claimed that Barak's "zone of immunity" warning did not mark "the first time that the Israelis have invented a phrase that suggests a hard deadline before an attack. At the end of the Bush administration, they said they could not allow Iran to go past 'the point of no return.' That phrase was also ill-defined, but seemed to suggest that once Iran had the know-how and the basic materials to make a bomb, it would be inevitable."[93] In that case, and in the current case as well, some observers have expressed opinions that the timetables are mainly intended to intimidate Iran and to prod the United States and other international actors into taking tougher and more urgent action.[94]

The issue of Israeli independent action is linked to U.S. attitudes and decisions. According to multiple sources, including the following excerpt from a February 2012 article, Israeli leaders have not been satisfied with U.S. responses to their attempts to obtain assurances that the United States would use force against Iran if non-military measures are deemed insufficient:

> One former Israeli official tells *Newsweek* he heard this explanation directly from Defense Minister Ehud Barak. "If Israel will miss its last opportunity [to attack], then we will have to lean only on the United States, and if the United States decides not to attack, then we will face an Iran with a bomb," says the former Israeli official. This source says that Israel has asked Obama for assurances that if sanctions fail, he will use force against Iran. Obama's refusal to provide that assurance has helped shape Israel's posture: a refusal to promise restraint, or even to give the United States advance notice.[95]

It is unclear whether the Israelis might be willing to reconsider this posture in the wake of Netanyahu's meeting with President Obama and other U.S. officials in March 2012. Amos Yadlin, a former head of Israeli military intelligence and one of the Israel Air Force pilots who carried out the 1981 Osirak strike, has been quoted as saying, "The US has promised not to allow Iran to have the bomb, but can Israel rely on this promise? That is the key to what Israel may decide to do."[96]

Military Action Versus Alternative Courses of Action

It is unclear how Israeli officials might react to Obama Administration efforts to convince them to give more time for sanctions with increasingly broad multilateral support to take fuller effect before elevating military options to the fore.[97] An Israeli investigative reporter quoted a "very

---

(...continued)

bomb and three years before testing one." "Attacking Iran: Up in the air," *Economist*, February 25, 2012.

[92] Colin H. Kahl, "An Israeli strike on Iran would backfire," *Washington Post*, March 4, 2012.

[93] Landler and Sanger, op. cit.

[94] Tobias Buck, "Israel debate on Iran strike gains urgency," *Financial Times*, February 3, 2012.

[95] Klaidman, et al., op. cit. See also "Israel wouldn't warn U.S. before Iran strike, says intelligence source," *Associated Press*, February 28, 2012; Bergman, "Will Israel Attack Iran?", op. cit.

[96] Susser, op. cit.

[97] Klaidman, et al., op. cit.

senior Israeli security source" as saying that "Americans tell us there is time, and we tell them that they only have about six to nine months more than we do and that therefore the sanctions have to be brought to a culmination now, in order to exhaust that track."[98]

In late 2011 and early 2012, the United States and the European Union (EU) imposed sanctions—due to take effect in June and July, respectively—aimed directly at Iran's export of crude oil, which accounts for around 70% of its hard currency revenue.[99] Many Israeli officials acknowledge that sanctions have begun to significantly affect Iran's economy.[100] That effect could be compounded following the March 2012 expulsion by the Brussels-based SWIFT (Society for Worldwide International Financial Transfers) of all Iranian banks blacklisted by the EU from its electronic transfer system. It is not clear, however, how a sustained, intensifying economic impact on the Iranian regime and its people could affect the regime's behavior or policy, including with regard to a possible return to international diplomacy.[101] In early March, the "P5+1" (United States, United Kingdom, France, Germany, China, and Russia) accepted Iran's proposal to restart negotiations in the spring of 2012 on its nuclear program. Israeli Vice Prime Minister and Strategic Affairs Minister Moshe Ya'alon was quoted as saying in March that the spring 2012 talks between Iran and the P5+1 would show "if there is a chance that the sanctions are working or that the Iranians are continuing to manoeuvre and advance toward a military nuclear capability."[102]

It is also unclear to what extent Israelis believe that their alleged ongoing covert action or "secret war" against Iran's nuclear program[103] might mitigate the need for an air strike. The two most recently retired heads of the Mossad, Meir Dagan and Ephraim Halevy, have both publicly stated that an Israeli military strike against Iran's nuclear facilities would be counterproductive, partly because they both reportedly "believe sabotage and diplomacy have done much to set back Iran's nuclear ambitions and can do more yet."[104] Dagan has been quoted as saying, "The Iranian problem must be shaped as an international problem, and efforts to delay Iran's nuclear program should continue."[105] In March 2012, Vice Prime Minister Ya'alon was quoted as saying, when asked if Israel might be just weeks away from a strike on Iran, "No. Look, we have to see. The [Iranian nuclear] project is not static.... Sometimes there are explosions, sometimes there are

---

[98] Bergman, "Will Israel Attack Iran?", op. cit.

[99] For more information on Iran sanctions and their effects, see CRS Report RS20871, *Iran Sanctions*, by Kenneth Katzman.

[100] Buck, op. cit.

[101] For two U.S. perspectives on this question, see Dennis B. Ross, "Iran is Ready to Talk," *New York Times*, February 14, 2012; Gerald F. Seib, "Iran Is Becoming Election Wild Card," *Wall Street Journal*, February 28, 2012.

[102] Dan Williams, "Israel says sabotage may stretch Iran atom timeline," *Reuters*, March 27, 2012.

[103] Melman, "The war against Iran's nuclear program has already begun," op. cit.

[104] Bruce Riedel, "The Israeli Anti-Attack-Iran Brigade," *The Daily Beast*, November 7, 2011.

[105] Quote from Israeli newspaper *Yedioth Ahronoth* translated in "Former Mossad chief against Iran strike," *United Press International*, May 8, 2011. An Israeli analyst has suggested a wider array of options short of a preemptive strike: "As the Iranian regime works hard to get nuclear weapons and missiles capable of carrying them, Israel uses the time to build a multi-level defensive and offensive capability. These layers include: U.S. early warning stations and anti-missile missile installations in the Gulf; Israeli missile-launching submarines; Israeli long-range planes whose crews have rehearsed and planned for strikes at Iranian facilities; different types of anti-missile missiles capable of knocking down the small number of missiles Iran could fire simultaneously; covert operations, possibly including computer viruses and assassinations, to slow down Iran's development of nuclear weapons; improved intelligence; help to the Iranian opposition (though the idea of "regime change" in the near future is a fantasy); and other measures." Rubin, op. cit.

worms there, viruses, all kinds of things like that."[106] However, according to one report from an Israeli investigative journalist, some senior Israeli military intelligence officials believe that—as was the case with Iraq's nuclear program in the late 1970s/early 1980s—possible Mossad actions have not stopped Iran's progress toward nuclear weapons capability.[107]

---

[106] Ya'alon quoted and translated from Israel's Army Radio in Williams, op. cit.

[107] Bergman, "Will Israel Attack Iran?", op. cit.

The Israeli Decisionmaking Process[108]

Several factors may influence any Israeli political decision relating to a possible strike on Iranian nuclear facilities. These include, but are not limited to, the views and interactions of Israeli decisionmakers; the public debate in Israel, the stances and anticipated responses of U.S., regional, and international actors; estimates of the effects of a possible strike; and the anticipated Iranian response regionally and internationally.

Discussion below regarding the Israeli decisionmaking process and the factors that may influence it is largely dependent on secondary sources that CRS does not claim to confirm independently.

Decisionmakers: Views and Interactions

According to one report, the issue of a possible Israeli strike on Iran has "sparked fierce public debate in Israel among political and military leaders, past and present, dividing cabinet ministers, generals and Mossad chiefs. Most see military action as a last resort to be contemplated only if sanctions and diplomacy fail; others insist that bombing Iran could actually stabilize the Middle East by setting back the radical cause indefinitely."[111]

> **The Security Cabinet and "Octet"**
>
> Israel's security cabinet is the group of government ministers convened by the prime minister to make decisions on matters related to national security.[109] The prime minister can have outside security and military officials brief the group. Prime ministers also rely upon security cabinet majorities to confirm broad-based support within Israel's coalition-based parliamentary democracy for important courses of action.
>
> During the tenure of this government, Prime Minister Netanyahu has tended to convene and rely upon the opinions of a smaller group of eight ministers within the security cabinet, known as the "octet," perhaps partly due to concerns that larger groups are more prone to leaking information publicly.[110]
>
> Current security cabinet (first eight comprise octet)
> **Binyamin Netanyahu (Prime Minister)**
> **Ehud Barak (Defense Minister/Deputy PM)**
> **Avigdor Lieberman (Foreign Minister/Deputy PM)**
> **Moshe Ya'alon (Vice PM/Strategic Affairs Minister)**
> **Yuval Steinitz (Finance Minister)**
> **Eli Yishai (Interior Minister/Deputy PM)**
> **Dan Meridor (Intel. & Atomic Ener. Min./Dep. PM)**
> **Benny Begin (Minister without Portfolio)**
> **Silvan Shalom (Vice PM/Regional Dev. Minister)**
> **Yitzhak Aharonovitch (Internal Security Minister)**
> **Yaakov Ne'eman (Justice Minister)**
> **Gideon Sa'ar (Education Minister)**
> **Uzi Landau (National Infrastructure Minister)**
> **Ariel Atias (Housing & Construction Minister)**

A 2011 RAND Corporation report cited a former Israeli official as saying that "the majority of ministers currently in power (including Prime Minister Netanyahu) would support military action to avoid Iran's acquiring a bomb under

---

[108] Prepared by Jim Zanotti, Specialist in Middle Eastern Affairs.

[109] A February 2012 report quoted Israeli Vice Prime Minister and Strategic Affairs Minister Moshe Ya'alon as saying, "In the State of Israel, any process of a military operation, and any military move, undergoes the approval of the security cabinet and in certain cases, the full cabinet." Jeffrey Heller and Dan Williams, "Prime Minister Netanyahu can't fly solo in Israel to attack Iran," *Reuters*, February 7, 2012. The security cabinet of Menachem Begin reportedly elected to carry out the 1981 strike on Iraq's Osirak nuclear reactor over the objections of the then Mossad director, and the security cabinet of Ehud Olmert reportedly supported the 2007 strike against Syria's presumed nuclear reactor under construction at Al Kibar (near Deir al Zur) by a vote of 13-1. For additional information on how the decisionmaking process on Iran might proceed under Prime Minister Netanyahu, see a transcript of an interview with the former director-general of Netanyahu's office in Dovid Efune, "On Iran and Obama, How Bibi will Decide – Exclusive Interview with Eyal Gabbai, Part 1" *The Algemeiner*, March 5, 2012.

[110] Eli Lake, "Meet the Israeli 'Octet' That Would Decide an Iran Attack," *Daily Beast*, March 9, 2012.

[111] Susser, op. cit.

---

their watch."[112] However, an Israeli journalist known for covering intelligence issues wrote in February 2012 that "as [former Mossad chief Meir] Dagan, the majority of Israeli Cabinet ministers, the CIA, and others have made clear, there is no need to strike in the near future since there is still time before Iran produces its first bomb."[113]

In a January 2012 interview, Defense Minister Barak indicated that there were "three categories of questions, which he characterized as 'Israel's ability to act,' 'international legitimacy' and 'necessity,' all of which require affirmative responses before a decision is made to attack:"

> 1. Does Israel have the ability to cause severe damage to Iran's nuclear sites and bring about a major delay in the Iranian nuclear project? And can the military and the Israeli people withstand the inevitable counterattack?
>
> 2. Does Israel have overt or tacit support, particularly from America, for carrying out an attack?
>
> 3. Have all other possibilities for the containment of Iran's nuclear threat been exhausted, bringing Israel to the point of last resort? If so, is this the last opportunity for an attack?[114]

Whether Israel's leaders believe the answer is "yes" or "no" to each of these three questions is a subject of debate among U.S. and Israeli analysts. A January 2012 *New York Times* article stated that

> conversations with eight current and recent top Israeli security officials suggested several things: since Israel has been demanding the new sanctions, including an oil embargo and seizure of Iran's Central Bank assets, it will give the sanctions some months to work; the sanctions are viewed here as probably insufficient; a military attack remains a very real option; and [post-attack] situations are considered less perilous than one in which Iran has nuclear weapons.[115]

In Israeli policymakers' evaluation of post-attack situations, however, one Israeli analyst asserted in February 2012 that they are so focused on the "immediate military implications" that they

> are ignoring several of the potential longer-term aspects of a strike: the preparedness of Israel's home front; the contours of an Israeli exit strategy; the impact on U.S.-Israel relations; the global diplomatic fallout; the stability of world energy markets; and the outcome within Iran itself. Should Israel fail to openly debate and account for these factors in advance of an attack, it may end up with a strategic debacle, even if it achieves its narrow military goals.[116]

Israeli sources indicate that top leaders are divided on the issue. One journalist asserted in February that Netanyahu's and Barak's apparent support for an attack in the near future is countered by many cabinet ministers and security establishment officials who supposedly share former Mossad chief Dagan's perspective "against a strike and in favor of sanctions and covert operations." That view is based at least partly on doubts about Israel's military capability to set

---

[112] Kaye et al., op. cit., p. 40.

[113] Yossi Melman, "Face Off," *Tablet*, February 9, 2012.

[114] Bergman, "Will Israel Attack Iran?", op. cit.

[115] Ethan Bronner, "Israel Senses Bluffing in Iran's Threats of Retaliation," *New York Times*, January 26, 2012.

[116] Ehud Eiran, "What Happens After Israel Attacks Iran," *foreignaffairs.com*, February 23, 2012.

back Iran's nuclear program three to five years.[117] According to a November 2011 article by another Israeli journalist:

> Benny Begin and Moshe Yaalon, two of the most hardline right-wing ministers in the "Octet Forum," the Israeli Cabinet's main decision-making body, are currently opposed to an attack because they believe a military strike will cause a massive backlash from Iran and its proxies and should only be a very last resort.[118]

According to the same article, "Netanyahu's decision to replace Dagan [in early 2011]—coupled with Barak's insistence on removing popular army chief [Gabi] Ashkenazi in February [2011]— was seen by many as an intentional strategy to remove opponents of a military strike on Iran from positions of influence."[119] In June 2011, the *New York Times* quoted Dagan as saying, "I decided to speak out because when I was in office, [former Israel Security Agency (Shin Bet) director Yuval] Diskin, Ashkenazi and I could block any dangerous adventure. Now I am afraid that there is no one to stop Bibi [Netanyahu] and Barak."[120] Despite changeovers in top Israeli security positions, an Israeli military correspondent was quoted as claiming in February 2012 that the current Israel Defense Forces Chief of Staff, Lieutenant General Benny Gantz, is considered a leader of a school of thought within the security establishment that reportedly has not concluded that the time has come for military action.[121] One report cited a former senior Israeli official as saying that the defense establishment "was not enthusiastic about an attack. It hoped that sanctions and diplomacy would work and that if military action were needed it would come from the United States."[122]

It is unclear how influential security officials' views would be in a decision on a strike. When an interviewer told Barak in January 2012 about top-ranking military personnel who argue that a military strike is either unnecessary or would be ineffective, Barak said, "It's good to have diversity in thinking and for people to voice their opinions. But at the end of the day, when the military command looks up, it sees us—the minister of defense and the prime minister. When we look up, we see nothing but the sky above us."[123] In mid March 2012, one report quoted an Israeli journalist as writing that a slight majority of Israel's security cabinet supports a strike:

> According to the most recent assessments, at this point eight ministers tend to support Netanyahu and Barak's position, while six object to it. It should be noted that the security

---

[117] Melman, "Face Off," op. cit.

[118] Anshel Pfeffer, "Will They?", *Tablet*, November 18, 2011. Israeli reports in early November 2011 about other "octet" members said that Foreign Minister Avigdor Lieberman had been convinced to support a strike on Iran, while Intelligence and Atomic Energy Minister Dan Meridor objected to an "immediate attack" and Interior Minister Eli Yishai had not made up his mind. Barak Ravid, et al., "Netanyahu trying to persuade cabinet to support attack on Iran," *Ha'aretz*, November 2, 2011; Ari Shavit, "Decision to attack Iran must be made with a clear mind," *Ha'aretz*, November 3, 2011.

[119] Pfeffer, "Will They?", op. cit. However, Dagan was one of the longest-serving Mossad directors (2002-2011), having had his term extended multiple times following his initial appointment, including once by Netanyahu.

[120] Ethan Bronner, "A Former Spy Chief Questions the Judgment of Israeli Leaders," *New York Times*, June 3, 2011.

[121] *Ha'aretz* journalist Amir Oren, quoted in Vita Bekker, "US worries grow over Israeli strike on Iran," *The National* (United Arab Emirates), February 20, 2012.

[122] Bronner, "Israel Senses Bluffing in Iran's Threats of Retaliation," op. cit.

[123] Bergman, "Will Israel Attack Iran?", op. cit.

cabinet has yet to hold a decisive meeting on the issue and the assessments are based on secret talks being held between the prime minister and his ministers, one at a time.[124]

Another mid March Israeli report claimed that "if Netanyahu and Minister of Defense, Ehud Barak, decide to attack, they'll be able to pass a decision through the cabinet without significant difficulty. With the exception of ministers Benny Begin and Dan Meridor, a tenacious objection against an Israeli strike on Iran is not expected."[125]

Some Israeli analysts question whether Netanyahu is likely to launch a strike against Iran. He has not ordered a major military offensive during either of his stints as Israel's prime minister (1996-1999 and 2009-present), possibly owing in part to what some analysts have observed to be a generally cautious approach to decisionmaking.[126] In his meeting with President Obama at the White House on March 5, 2012, Netanyahu reportedly confirmed that no decision had been made to that point.[127]

Yet, speaking at the annual American Israel Public Affairs Committee (AIPAC) conference in Washington, DC, on March 5, 2012, Netanyahu said:

> We've waited for diplomacy to work. We've waited for sanctions to work. None of us can afford to wait much longer. As Prime Minister of Israel, I will never let my people live under the shadow of annihilation. Some commentators would have you believe that stopping Iran from getting the bomb is more dangerous than letting Iran have the bomb. They say that a military confrontation with Iran would undermine the efforts already underway, that it would be ineffective, and that it would provoke even more vindictive action by Iran.

Netanyahu then referred to correspondence in 1944 between the World Jewish Congress and the U.S. government that apparently indicated U.S. unwillingness to bomb Auschwitz because of the "doubtful efficacy" of the operation and the possibility of "even more vindictive action by the Germans." In response to Netanyahu's speech, the editor-in-chief of Israel's *Ha'aretz* newspaper wrote:

> The Holocaust talk has but one meaning—forcing Israel to go to war and strike the Iranians.... No amount of missiles falling on Tel Aviv, rising oil prices and economic crises matter when compared to genocide.... Enough loopholes can be detected that would allow Netanyahu to escape an imminent decision to go to war.... Nevertheless, Netanyahu took on a public obligation on Monday that would make it very hard for him to back away from the path of war with Iran.[128]

---

[124] Excerpt from article by Ben Caspit in Israel's Hebrew-language *Ma'ariv* newspaper, translated and quoted in "Most of Israel security cabinet backs Iran strike," *Agence France Presse*, March 15, 2012.

[125] Amir Rapaport, "Who Opposes Attacking Iran," *Israel Defense*, March 16, 2012. For a report detailing the relationship between Netanyahu and Barak and their interaction on this issue, see Ethan Bronner, "2 Israeli Leaders Make Iran Issue Their Own," *New York Times*, March 27, 2012.

[126] CRS telephone interview with former Israeli deputy national security advisor and military planning director Brig. Gen. (ret.) Shlomo Brom, February 21, 2012. Daniel Levy, "Netanyahu Won't Attack Iran (Probably)," *foreignpolicy.com*, March 2, 2012.

[127] Barak Ravid, "Netanyahu tells Obama: I have yet to decide whether to attack Iran," *Ha'aretz*, March 6, 2012.

[128] Aluf Benn, "By conjuring the Holocaust, Netanyahu brought Israel closer to war with Iran," *haaretz.com*, March 6, 2012.

In early March 2012 interviews on Israeli television following his Washington, DC, trip, Netanyahu reportedly said:

> This is not a matter of days or weeks. It is also not a matter of years. The result has to be that the threat of a nuclear weapon in Iran's hands is removed…. If you don't make the decision, and you don't succeed in preventing it, who will you explain that [to]? To historians? To the generations that were here before us? To the generations that won't come after us? It is forbidden to let the Iranians get nuclear arms. And I intend not to allow that to happen.[129]

Public Opinion and Debate in Israel

A U.S.-based Israeli analyst has noted that domestic Israeli political factors might militate against Netanyahu undertaking the risks a strike would entail—including his coalition's apparently strong prospects for reelection in 2012 or 2013, and a reported lack of pressure for military action on Iran from the public or from coalition partners seen as having generally hawkish views.[130] Public opinion polls conducted in February and March 2012 indicated reluctance by a majority of Israelis to support an attack on Iranian nuclear facilities in the absence of U.S. cooperation. Assuming an Israeli attack without U.S. cooperation, a mid March poll conducted jointly by Israeli and Palestinian organizations indicated that Israelis would oppose a strike by a 51%-42% margin. A sizeable majority, however, would apparently support an attack with U.S. cooperation by a 69%-26% margin.[131] An Israeli political science professor involved with a late February poll on the same questions reportedly explained the Israeli views as follows: "They are not challenging the right to [attack], [they are] challenging the ability to do it effectively and with international support. People don't want Israel to become the troublemaker of the world."[132]

A public debate in which Israeli officials and non-government analysts might engage appears to be a controversial subject in its own right. According to one report, "No issue in Israel is more fraught than the debate over the wisdom and feasibility of a strike on Iran…. Security officials are increasingly kept from journalists or barred from discussing Iran. Much of the public talk is as much message delivery as actual policy."[133] In a November 2011 poll taken by Israel's Dialog polling institute, Israelis indicated by a 51%-39% margin that they oppose public discussion of a possible attack because it could "cause damage."[134]

---

[129] Prime Minister Netanyahu quoted in Herb Keinon, "Netanyahu: Attack on Iran not immediately in offing," *jpost.com*, March 8, 2012.

[130] Levy, op. cit. See also Paul Pillar, "Why Israeli Public Opinion Opposes a Strike on Iran," *theatlantic.com*, March 1, 2012.

[131] Poll of 600 adult Israelis during the period of March 11-15, 2012, conducted by the Harry S. Truman Research Institute for the Advancement of Peace at the Hebrew University of Jerusalem and the Palestinian Center for Policy and Survey Research in Ramallah, West Bank. Details of the poll, which has a margin of error of 4.5%, are available at http://www.pcpsr.org/survey/polls/2012/p43ejoint.html. A late February poll conducted by Israel's Dahaf Institute indicated that Israelis would oppose a strike without U.S. cooperation by a 63%-31% margin, and support a strike with U.S. cooperation by a 62%-34% margin. See http://www.peaceindex.org/indexMonthEng.aspx?num=240#anchor269. A poll taken by Israel's Dialog polling institute in early March indicated only 26% support for an independent Israeli strike. See http://www.imra.org.il/story.php3?id=55988.

[132] Tel Aviv University professor Tamar Herrmann, quoted in Joshua Mitnick, "Majority of Israelis oppose a unilateral strike on Iran nuclear program," *Christian Science Monitor*, March 8, 2012.

[133] Bronner, "Israel Senses Bluffing in Iran's Threats of Retaliation," op. cit.

[134] Details of the poll, which has a margin of error of 4.6%, are available at http://www.imra.org.il/story.php3?id=54362.

Some Israeli commentators have voiced concern that the public is resigned to the possibility of war with Iran, based on a tradition of deference to national leaders.[135] According to one commentator, "The impression is that the majority of Israelis are not afraid…. The decision is left up to a handful of people who have decided that the public, as usual, trusts them blindly, obediently."[136] An early March 2012 Dialog poll indicated that by a 50%-38% margin Israelis trust Netanyahu and Barak on the Iran issue.[137]

Two January 2012 articles co-authored by three Israeli analysts (including two former officials) argued that "a public discussion will assist those officials who are authorized to make informed decisions on this issue."[138] Both articles acknowledged the limitations of such a discussion given the apparent centrality to decisionmakers' considerations of classified information on Iran's nuclear program and on the operational capacity of Israel's air force. Yet, they still argued for a debate to proceed:

> Instead, the public debate must focus on the strategic dimensions of the issue—a realm in which civilian strategists have much to contribute. Indeed, airing these dimensions is an absolute imperative. Without it we are condemned to repeat the mistakes of the past or to commit worse ones. More important, without such airing we are doomed to step mindlessly closer and closer to a military confrontation with Iran or, possibly just as dangerous, to accept and accommodate its nuclear ambitions and designs.[139]

---

[135] Joel Greenberg, "Sense of inevitable war grips Israel," *Washington Post*, February 23, 2012; Larry Derfner, "Israel's Silent March to War with Iran," *Jewish Daily Forward*, February 10, 2012.

[136] Gideon Levy, "Israelis should be afraid of their leaders, not Iran," *Ha'aretz*, February 5, 2012.

[137] Details of the poll, which has a margin of error of 4.5%, are available at http://www.imra.org.il/story.php3?id=55988.

[138] Stein, et al., "The Public Discussion of Israel's Strategy Regarding a Nuclear Iran," op. cit. See also Shlomo Brom, Shai Feldman, Shimon Stein, "A real debate about Iran," *mideast.foreignpolicy.com*, January 30, 2012.

[139] Brom, et al., "A real debate about Iran," op. cit.

Potential Factors in an Israeli Decision: Stances and Anticipated Responses Outside Israel[140]

The United States

Despite the reference by Defense Minister Barak to the possible need for "overt or tacit support, particularly from America" before approving an Israel strike, it is unclear to what extent Israeli decisionmakers might be influenced by the stated positions and anticipated responses of U.S.

policymakers in the Obama Administration and Congress regarding an attack. Not surprisingly, Israeli leaders are extremely sensitive to U.S. views for a variety of reasons, including but not limited to:

- Strong U.S.-Israel relations dating back to when the United States was the first country to recognize the provisional Jewish government as the de facto government of Israel upon its declaration of statehood in May 1948;

- Robust ongoing military and security cooperation, including significant U.S. arms sales and other forms of support; and

- Trade ties and important bilateral economic and scientific cooperation.[141]

Israeli leaders' perspectives about the possible effects of a strike on U.S. political and material assistance to Israel, possible negative security consequences for the United States from a potential Iranian retaliation, and the probability of future U.S. military

---

Selected Polls of U.S. Views on Potential Israeli Strike

These poll results are included to provide information regarding U.S. public opinion on the issue, which could impact U.S. policymakers' views and positions and ultimately influence Israeli decisionmaking.

Reuters/Ipsos Public Affairs (March 8-11, 2012)
Do you support or oppose Israel taking military action against Iran if there is evidence that Iran is building nuclear weapons?
Strongly support: 40%, Somewhat support: 22%, Somewhat oppose: 11%, Strongly oppose: 19%, Neither: 4%, Unsure: 4%
(Poll of 1,084 adults with 3.1% margin of error)

CBS News/New York Times (March 7-11, 2012)
If Israel were to attack Iran in order to prevent it from developing a nuclear weapons program, should the U.S. support Israel's military action, or should the U.S. not get involved?
Support: 47%, Not get involved: 42%, Oppose (volunteered response): 1%, Unsure: 10%
(Poll of 1,009 adults with 3% margin of error)

ABC News/Washington Post (March 7-10, 2012)
Would you support or oppose Israel bombing Iran's nuclear development sites?
Support: 42%, Oppose: 51%, No opinion: 7%
(Poll of 1,003 adults with 4% margin of error)

Program on International Policy Attitudes/University of Maryland (March 3-7, 2012)
Do you think the U.S. should...
Discourage Israel from attacking Iran's nuclear program: 34%
Take a neutral stance: 46%
Encourage Israel to attack Iran's nuclear program: 14%
Don't know/Refused: 6%
(Poll of 727 Americans with 4.5% margin of error)

***The Hill*/Pulse Opinion Research** (March 1, 2012)
Support or oppose Israel attack on Iran to destroy nuclear program?
Very supportive: 28%, Somewhat supportive: 24%, Somewhat opposed: 22%, Very opposed: 19%, Not sure: 8%
(Poll of 1,000 likely voters with 3% margin of error)

---

[140] Prepared by Jim Zanotti, Specialist in Middle Eastern Affairs.

[141] For more details on these interactions, see CRS Report RL33476, *Israel: Background and U.S. Relations*, by Jim Zanotti; and CRS Report RL33222, *U.S. Foreign Aid to Israel* , by Jeremy M. Sharp.

action to prevent a nuclear-armed Iran may, among other considerations, influence the Israeli decisionmaking process

An Israeli journalist wrote in March 2012 that Israel did not ask permission when it acted to prevent Saddam Hussein and Bashar al Asad from obtaining nuclear weapons, but that "the [Obama] administration can credibly counter that in neither case did Israeli unilateralism threaten to draw America into an armed conflict, as it does now."[142] According to three Israeli analysts (including two former officials) mentioned above:

> Even after the withdrawal of its troops from Iraq, the U.S. remains extremely exposed to Iranian retaliation—either directly against its forces in the area or by Iran's attempting to ignite a broader conflict in the region—so an Israeli strike would harm U.S. interests in the region and would place many U.S. lives at risk. And while in an election year America's political reaction to such a strike may be mitigated by domestic political considerations, the reaction of the U.S. defense community to an Israeli military strike might be extremely negative, as such an action might be seen as representing Israeli insensitivity to and disregard of U.S. priorities and concerns.[143]

Some reports have speculated that an Israeli decision to attack, if it occurs, could come before the U.S. presidential election in November 2012, with one Israeli report stating, "A second-term president, not constrained by electoral necessities, will be able to apply a lot more pressure on the Israeli government not to attack."[144]

Separate from the question of whether the United States might support an Israeli strike on Iran, Israeli decisionmakers might be influenced by how they anticipate the United States would respond after an attack, including in the event of retaliation by Iran and its allies. Although the United States does not have a formal treaty obligation to defend Israel in the event it is attacked, successive Administrations have either stated or implied that the United States would act to protect Israel's security if it were endangered—including by Iran—and have worked with Congress to ensure and bolster Israel's "qualitative military edge" over regional security threats.[145]

---

[142] Yossi Klein Halevi, "Can Israel Trust the United States When It Comes to Iran?", *The New Republic*, March 2, 2012.

[143] Feldman, et al., "What to Do About Nuclearizing Iran? The Israeli Debate," op. cit.

[144] Anshel Pfeffer, "US election hands Netanyahu giant dilemma on Iran," *Jewish Chronicle Online*, February 9, 2012. See also Bret Stephens, "(How) Should Israel Bomb Iran," *Wall Street Journal*, February 7, 2012, stating, "Jerusalem knows that Mr. Obama will be hard-pressed to oppose an Israeli strike—the way Dwight Eisenhower did during the Suez crisis—before election day. A re-elected President Obama is a different story."

[145] For more information on the level of U.S. commitment to Israel's security, see CRS Report RL33476, *Israel: Background and U.S. Relations*, by Jim Zanotti; and CRS Report RL33222, *U.S. Foreign Aid to Israel* , by Jeremy M. Sharp. In addition to a Mutual Defense Assistance Agreement (TIAS 2675) dated July 23, 1952, the United States and Israel have entered into a range of stand-alone agreements, memoranda of understanding, and other arrangements varying in their formality. In remarks at the White House on March 5, 2012, with Prime Minister Netanyahu, the President said, "As I've said repeatedly, the bond between our two countries is unbreakable. My personal commitment—a commitment that is consistent with the history of other occupants of this Oval Office—our commitment to the security of Israel is rock solid. And as I've said to the Prime Minister in every single one of our meetings, the United States will always have Israel's back when it comes to Israel's security." In a March 2006 speech against the backdrop of Iran's hostile rhetoric toward Israel and pursuit of a nuclear program, President George W. Bush said, "I made it clear, I'll make it clear again, that we will use military might to protect our ally Israel." Seymour M. Hersh, "The Iran Plans," *The New Yorker*, April 17, 2006.

It is unclear to what extent U.S. expressions of willingness to act forcefully on Iran might encourage Israeli restraint. Since the second term of the George W. Bush Administration, U.S. officials have sought to maintain that a credible strike option exists while simultaneously communicating the possible risks for U.S. interests, regional security, and global energy markets if Israel were to act alone.[146] Addressing the AIPAC conference on March 4, 2012, President Obama said,

> Iran's leaders should have no doubt about the resolve of the United States—just as they should not doubt Israel's sovereign right to make its own decisions about what is required to meet its security needs.... Iran's leaders should know that I do not have a policy of containment; I have a policy to prevent Iran from obtaining a nuclear weapon.

An Israeli in Netanyahu's "inner circle" reportedly said in February that, compared with a year ago, President Obama's recent rhetoric indicates greater credibility that the United States would be "ready to attack if worse comes to worst,"[147] though it is not clear whether this provides reassurance at a level that might significantly affect Israeli leaders' calculations regarding the advisability of and need for independent action. In 2007, according to former President George W. Bush, Netanyahu's predecessor Ehud Olmert unsuccessfully sought U.S. action to destroy the secret Syrian reactor before he ordered the Israeli strike. President Bush said that he declined to order military action owing to the low confidence of the U.S. intelligence community that Syria had a nuclear weapons program, proposing—to Olmert's dismay—that they instead publicly expose the reactor's existence and pursue internationally backed coercive diplomacy.[148]

U.S. views have potential salience for Israeli decisionmakers because top Israeli officials do not necessarily agree with the Obama Administration on every aspect of how to address Iran's nuclear program. It is unclear, for example, to what extent views conveyed by President Obama and other U.S. officials in early 2012 that appear to appeal for more time to judge the effectiveness of international sanctions and diplomacy might affect Israeli positions on a possible strike. There are indications that Israeli officials continue to differ with the Obama Administration on points possibly relating to timeframes for action.[149] U.S. officials reportedly said in early March that the President "is not ready to accept a central part of Israel's strategic calculation: that an attack on Iran's nuclear facilities would be warranted to stop it from gaining the capability to build a nuclear weapon, rather than later, to stop it from actually manufacturing one."[150] The President and Netanyahu "did not close the gap on this issue" during their March 5 meeting, according to a U.S. official cited in one report who claimed that the issue was not addressed.[151]

---

[146] Eli Lake, "U.S., Israel Discuss Triggers for Bombing Iran's Nuclear Infrastructure," *Daily Beast*, December 28, 2011.

[147] Klaidman, et al., op. cit.

[148] George W. Bush, *Decision Points*, New York: Crown Publishers, 2010, pp. 421-422.

[149] Some Members of Congress have explicitly supported the concept of possible Israeli military action against Iran without setting forth a specific timeframe. In May 2011, Congressman Louie Gohmert introduced H.Res. 271, entitled: "Expressing support for the State of Israel's right to defend Israeli sovereignty, to protect the lives and safety of the Israeli people, and to use all means necessary to confront and eliminate nuclear threats posed by the Islamic Republic of Iran, including the use of military force if no other peaceful solution can be found within reasonable time to protect against such an immediate and existential threat to the State of Israel." To date, H.Res. 271 has 69 Republican co-sponsors and was referred to the House Foreign Affairs Subcommittee on the Middle East and South Asia.

[150] Mark Landler, "Israel's Backers Pressure Obama on Iran Position," *New York Times*, March 4, 2012.

[151] Mark Landler, "Obama Presses Israel to Resist Strikes on Iran," *New York Times*, March 6, 2012.

In a February 19, 2012, CNN interview, General Martin Dempsey, Chairman of the Joint Chiefs of Staff, revealed apparent differences in Israeli and U.S. positions, saying:

> we think that it's not prudent at this point to decide to attack Iran. I mean, that's been our counsel to our allies, the Israelis, well-known, well-documented.... I wouldn't suggest, sitting here today, that we've persuaded them that our view is the correct view and that they are acting in an ill-advised fashion, but we've had a very candid, collaborative conversation.[152]

In testimony before the Senate Budget Committee on February 28, General Dempsey explained his CNN remarks by saying, "I didn't counsel Israel not to attack. We've had a conversation with them about time, the issue of time." Further to the question of timing, President Obama said in an interview less than a week before the March 5 meeting with Netanyahu that "at a time when there is not a lot of sympathy for Iran and its only real ally [Syria] is on the ropes, do we want a distraction in which suddenly Iran can portray itself as a victim, and deflect attention from what has to be the core issue, which is their potential pursuit of nuclear weapons?"[153] A U.S. European Command-Israel joint missile defense exercise planned for April 2012—known as Austere Challenge 12—was postponed and has been rescheduled for later in 2012. Some reports claim that the postponement is at least partly intended to discourage perceptions of joint U.S.-Israel planning with respect to a possible early 2012 Israeli attack on Iran.[154]

During his March 2012 Washington, DC, trip, Prime Minister Netanyahu explicitly insisted on Israel's prerogative to act independently. In his March 5 AIPAC speech, Netanyahu said:

> Israel must always have the ability to defend itself, by itself, against any threat. We deeply appreciate the great alliance between our two countries. But when it comes to Israel's survival, we must always remain the masters of our fate.

After Netanyahu reportedly met in private with various congressional leaders during his trip to Washington, DC, on March 6, 2012, Senator Carl Levin, Chairman of the Senate Armed Services Committee, was quoted as saying that if Iran does not follow international demands that it stop uranium enrichment, "an attack on them by Israel is very likely."[155] Referring to Netanyahu's U.S. meetings following his return to Israel, his spokesman reportedly said, "A red light was not given. And if we're already talking about colors, then a green light was not given either."[156] In a March 14 speech in the Knesset addressing the issue, Netanyahu cited past decisions by Israeli leaders—the 1948 declaration of statehood, the initiation of the 1967 Arab-Israeli war, and the 1981 strike on Osirak—that were supposedly undertaken either without U.S. knowledge or despite prior counsel from U.S. officials to delay action.[157]

---

[152] Transcript of interview with General Martin Dempsey on CNN's *Fareed Zakaria GPS*, February 19, 2012.

[153] Goldberg, "Obama to Iran and Israel...," op. cit.

[154] Yaakov Katz, "Joint drill with US to be held after delay," *Jerusalem Post*, February 6, 2012.

[155] Donna Cassata, "Sen. Levin says Israeli attack on Iran likely," *Associated Press*, March 6, 2012.

[156] Netanyahu spokesman Liran Dan quoted in "Israel cautiously welcomes Western nuclear talks with Iran," *Reuters*, March 7, 2012.

[157] Transcript of English translation of speech (from Hebrew) available on Israeli Prime Minister's Office website.

Regionally and Internationally

It is unclear to what degree Israeli decisionmakers might take into account the anticipated reactions of other regional and international actors. Some Israeli analysts voice concern—given the possibility that a possible Israeli attack would not be sanctioned in advance by an international legal or political mandate[158]—about possible damage to Israel's growing political and economic relations with key countries such as China and Russia and potential acceleration of its international isolation or "delegitimization."[159] In 1981, the United Nations Security Council—including the United States under the Reagan Administration—voted unanimously in favor of Resolution 487, which condemned Israel's strike on Iraq's Osirak reactor as a violation of the U.N. Charter and the "norms of international conduct." Nevertheless, some of these same analysts suggest that if an Israeli attack successfully delays Iran's nuclear program without resulting in significant costs to other countries, "there might be quite a few regional and international players who in retrospect would be pleased that Israel took on itself the risks to solve the problem of Iranian nuclearization."[160]

It is not clear how other Middle Eastern actors' potential reactions might be affected by ongoing political change that may lead Arab governments to become more responsive to popular sentiment that includes anti-Israel strains. Israeli decisionmakers might be weighing the possible consequences of further alienating neighboring Arab states with which Israel has always had problematic relations. Doing so could possibly increase prospects for greater regional conflict, decrease chances for diplomatic progress on the Palestinian issue, and harm the U.S. regional profile.

---

[158] In one view, Yale law and political science professor Bruce Ackerman has argued that if "President Obama supports Netanyahu's preemptive strike, he will transform Bush's Iraq aberration into the founding precedent of a new era of international law. He should instead reaffirm Reagan's position in 1981 [joining the unanimous U.N. Security Council vote on Resolution 487, which found Israel's Osirak strike to be in violation of the U.N. Charter] and return the presidency to its traditional commitments to international law abroad and constitutional fidelity at home." Bruce Ackerman, "The legal case against attacking Iran," *Los Angeles Times*, March 5, 2012. In another view, Peter Berkowitz, a fellow at Stanford University's Hoover Institution, has argued, partly in light of what he characterizes as changing views on the imminence of national security threats in a post-9/11 world, that many considerations "separately, and certainly taken together, furnish legal justification, grounded in the right of anticipatory self-defense, for Israel or the United States to strike Iran's nuclear facilities. However, not everything that is lawful is prudent and wise." Peter Berkowitz, "Would a Military Strike Against Iran Be Legal?", *RealClearPolitics*, March 4, 2012. The IAEA General Conference adopted a resolution in 1985 (GC(29)/RES/444) considering that an "armed attack on and threat against nuclear facilities devoted to peaceful purposes constitutes a violation of the principles of the United Nations Charter, international law and the Statute of the Agency," and adopted a resolution in 1990 (GC(34)/RES/533) encouraging all IAEA member states to be ready to provide immediate peaceful assistance—if requested—to countries whose safeguarded facilities have been attacked.

[159] Stein, et al., "The Public Discussion of Israel's Strategy Regarding a Nuclear Iran," op. cit. Israel claims that its detractors—some of whom it claims are motivated by anti-Israel or anti-Semitic convictions—seek to delegitimize its international standing, often by exaggerating alleged human rights and international law violations regarding its actions vis-à-vis Palestinians in the West Bank and the Gaza Strip.

[160] Ibid.

Potential Factors in an Israeli Decision: Possible Operational Aspects of an Israeli Strike[161]

Another factor in Israel's deliberations is the question of operational capability: Can Israeli forces conduct a successful strike, however they define "success"? One Israeli journalist has written:

> While a large-scale operation against Iran ... would stretch the [Israel Air Force's] resources, it is still within its capabilities. This is exactly what the lion's share of the defense budget has been spent on for over more than a decade. On fighter jets, airborne tankers, long-range reconnaissance drones and electronic warfare aircraft.[162]

According to another Israeli report, "military thinkers acknowledge the objective difficulties but argue that, with the out-of-the-box improvisation and planning the Israel Air Force is renowned for, they can be surmounted."[163] Not all Israeli assessments agree, however. One Israeli analyst has written:

> Would such an attack by Israel be likely to succeed even in doing maximum damage to Iranian facilities? No, a great deal could go wrong, especially against multiple hardened targets at the planes' maximum range. Planes could get lost or crash or have to turn back. Planes arriving over the targets could miss, or accidentally drop their bombs on civilians, or simply not do much damage. Many targets would remain unscathed.[164]

A senior Israeli official was cited in one report as quoting a senior commander who reportedly told the Israeli cabinet in September 2011 that "we have no ability to hit the Iranian nuclear program in a meaningful way."[165] A March 2012 poll indicated that 65% of Jewish Israelis believe that the Israeli military has the "ability to damage Iran's nuclear program substantially,"[166] while a late February 2012 poll indicated by a 53%-39% margin that Jewish Israelis do not believe that an Israeli attack conducted without U.S. cooperation would stop "Iran's nuclearization for a substantial period of time."[167]

In open source assessments mainly in non-Israeli media, analysts assert that although the Israel Air Force (IAF) is formidable, an attempt to destroy Iran's nuclear capability would be a challenge due to both the IAF's technical capabilities and the limited numbers of aircraft in its fleet that are equipped to simultaneously operate over long ranges, carry the necessary ordnance, and thwart foreign air defenses. Former Central Intelligence Agency and National Security Agency Director Michael Hayden said, for example, "that airstrikes capable of seriously setting

---

[161] Prepared by Jeremiah Gertler, Specialist in Military Aviation.

[162] Anshel Pfeffer, "Israel could strike Iran's nuclear facilities, but it won't be easy," *haaretz.com*, February 20, 2012.

[163] Susser, op. cit.

[164] Rubin, op. cit.

[165] Vick, op. cit. Following this quote, the article states, "The key word is *meaningful* [emphasis original]. The working assumption behind Israel's military preparations has been that a strike, to be worth mounting, must delay Tehran's nuclear capabilities by at least two years." Ibid.

[166] Poll of 505 Jewish Israelis conducted by Professor Camil Fuchs of Tel Aviv University for the Jerusalem Center for Public Affairs. Details of the poll, whose margin of error is unspecified, available at http://jcpa.org/JCPA/Templates/ShowPage.asp?DBID=1&LNGID=1&TMID=111&FID=254&PID=0&IID=13295.

[167] Dahaf Institute poll, February 28-29, 2012, with a 4.5% margin of error, details available at http://www.peaceindex.org/indexMonthEng.aspx?num=240#anchor269.

back Iran's nuclear program were 'beyond the capacity' of Israel."[168] Multiple reports have asserted that military analysts believe that reaching all critical Iranian nuclear facilities "would require an air campaign of hundreds of sorties and would have to last for weeks."[169] However, a U.S. defense analyst has said that any Israeli attack would probably be a one-time event: "Given the unfriendly airspace Israeli strike aircraft would have to traverse to reach Iran's facilities as well as Israel's geographic distance from Iran, the likelihood of Israel being able to carry out repeated strikes is low. Israeli strike aircraft would only have one opportunity to strike at Iran's nuclear facilities."[170] Nevertheless, the same defense analyst has said, "One wave can do a lot, depending on the quality of the penetrating munitions and the targeting abilities."[171]

Access

The distance from Israeli bases to Iranian nuclear facilities imposes two significant difficulties. The first involves airspace. Depending on the route selected, Israeli aircraft would have to cross the sovereign airspace of Saudi Arabia, Jordan, Iraq, Syria, and/or Turkey both en route and on the return trip. According to one report, "The route over Iraq would be the most direct and likely, defense analysts say, because Iraq effectively has no air defenses and the United States, after its December withdrawal, no longer has the obligation to defend Iraqi skies."[172]

Each route involves different diplomatic considerations, but Israel has shown a willingness and ability to operate in foreign airspace for limited periods with little or no detection and without targeting air defense sites, as in the 2007 raid on the suspected Syrian nuclear site near Deir al Zur.[173] However, although Israel may be able to hide comparatively small combat aircraft from foreign air defense systems through electronic and other means, large tankers and other support aircraft required for a long-range strike on Iran may be another matter. According to a 2010 book by two U.S. analysts, "It seems likely that Jordan, Saudi Arabia, and Kuwait would be able to detect the overflight of Israeli aircraft. Syria might not see ingressing aircraft, but the ability to blind the Syrians again, after doing so in 2007, is not something Israel can take for granted."[174]

Although there have been past reports—officially denied—that Saudi Arabia has granted or would grant advance permission for Israel to overfly its territory,[175] Israel may rely on

---

[168] Elisabeth Bumiller, "Iran Raid Seen as a Huge Task for Israeli Jets," *New York Times*, February 19, 2012.

[169] Vick, op. cit. See also General (USAF ret.) Charles Wald, in Jim Michaels, "Israeli Attack On Iran Would Be Complex," *USA Today*, February 14, 2012.

[170] Anthony H. Cordesman, *The New IAEA Report And Iran's Evolving Nuclear And Missile Forces*, Center for Strategic and International Studies, November 8, 2011.

[171] Vick, op. cit.

[172] Bumiller, "Iran Raid Seen as a Huge Task for Israeli Jets," op. cit.

[173] An article by former German Defense Ministry director of planning (1982-1988) Hans Rühle for Switzerland's *Neuer Zürcher Zeitung* on the 2007 Syria raid claimed that seven Israeli F-15s "flew along the Mediterranean coast, brushed past Turkey and pressed on into Syria. Fifty kilometers (30 miles) from their target they fired 22 rockets at the three identified objects inside the Kibar complex." Article translated and quoted in "Iranian defector tipped Syrian nuke plans," *Associated Press*, March 19, 2009. In the 1981 strike on Iraq's Osirak reactor, the eight Israeli F-16s that carried out the bombing and six supporting F-15s transited Jordanian and Saudi airspace en route and on the return trip. An overflight of present-day Jordan might have more complicated political ramifications, given that Israel and Jordan signed a peace treaty in 1994.

[174] Allin and Simon, op. cit., p. 99.

[175] Hugh Tomlinson, "Saudi Arabia gives Israel clear skies to attack Iranian nuclear sites," *The Times* (UK), June 12, 2010.

---

technological and logistical advantages mentioned in the above paragraph to elude interception during its overflight of third-party countries. Additionally, according to a book by two U.S. analysts, "For all these countries except Syria, the balance of incentives might well lie on the side of silence … a humbled Iran would be the overriding interest, especially if intercepting aircraft were likely to be shot to pieces by Israeli fighters."[176] Active resistance to Israeli overflight using surface-to-air missiles or intercepting aircraft could, at a minimum, derail Israel's "intricate attack plan"[177]—for example, by lengthening Israeli flight routes and complicating refueling plans.

A second challenge is that the distance to targets and the size of a possible strike package would require all of Israel's aerial refueling capability, with little or no margin for equipment or operational failures. A February 2012 *Economist* article anticipated the facilities that an Israeli strike might target:

> Israel would probably pay particular attention to the enrichment plants at Natanz and Fordow; after them would come the facility at Isfahan that turns uranium into a gas that the centrifuges can work with and the heavy-water reactor under construction at Arak, both of which are above the ground. The larger Russian-built reactor at Bushehr would probably escape unscathed; it is less relevant to weapons work and damage to it could spread contamination across the Gulf.[178]

See **Figure 1** for a map of major Iranian facilities in regional context. Israel has five KC-130s and four 707-based tankers similar to American KC-135s.[179] A 2009 study estimated a need for 12 tanker equivalents per mission simply to attack Iranian nuclear facilities at Esfahan, Natanz, and Arak (the Fordow facility had not yet been revealed).[180] Without additional tankers, the fighters would have to refuel twice over the duration of the mission. This need may be somewhat reduced by the fact that Israel is also believed to have "mastered the operation of 'buddy refueling,'" using the F-15s' drop tanks to refuel the shorter-range F-16s en route.[181] Additionally, one Israeli report states, "For the last few years, Israeli representatives have been snapping up every old Boeing 707 airliner in good condition … and converting them into airborne tankers. According to various sources, the IAF has by now eight or nine such tankers."[182]

Analysts differ in assessing the effectiveness of Iranian air defenses. Iran's defensive missile systems are among the least modern in the Middle East, relying on Hawk systems supplied by the United States before the Iranian Revolution and Vietnam-era Russian SA-2s, along with a few more modern SA-5s. But they are controlled, some argue, by a modern, coordinated network. One analyst has said, "They're not using wax pencils on glass…. [t]hey have updated

---

[176] Allin and Simon, op. cit., pp. 99-100.

[177] Ibid., p. 49.

[178] "Attacking Iran: Up in the air," op. cit. Former Deputy Assistant Secretary of Defense Colin Kahl has said that an Israeli attack might also target "multiple centrifuge production facilities in and around populated areas of Tehran and Natanz." Kahl, "An Israeli strike on Iran would backfire," op. cit.

[179] *The Military Balance 2011*, Chapter Seven: Middle East and North Africa, International Institute for Strategic Studies, March, 2011. Israel has supported distant deployments before, most notably a 2,600-kilometer deployment to Poland, albeit only three fighters were involved.

[180] Abdullah Toukan and Anthony H. Cordesman, *Study on a Possible Israeli Strike on Iran's Nuclear Development Facilities*, Center for Strategic & International Studies, Washington, DC, March 8, 2009.

[181] Hans Rühle, "Wie Israel Irans Atomprogramm zerstören könnte (How Israel could destroy Iran's nuclear program)," *Die Welt* (Germany), February 16, 2012 (CRS translation).

[182] Pfeffer, "Israel could strike Iran's nuclear facilities, but it won't be easy," op. cit.

---

computerized modern air defenses."[183] Another has raised the possibility, however slight, that Russia might have "in recent years secretly supplied [Iran] with the SA-12 Giant or the latest variants of the S-300 series" air defense systems.[184] If that is the case, analysts estimate that the attrition rate of Israeli aircraft in an air strike could be significantly higher than otherwise.[185]

Aircraft

Although an attack on Esfahan, Natanz, and Arak might require deploying only 20% of Israel's top-line fighters purchased from the United States, it would probably require 100% of the most capable—the IAF's 25 F-15Is.[186] Undertaking additional strikes on Fordow and possibly other facilities—such as those related to research, centrifuge production, uranium mining and processing, or even possible weapons production—would probably require diverting some of these aircraft from the first three targets and possibly addressing some targets through alternative means (see below). According to a Center for Strategic and International Studies (CSIS) report, "Israeli aircraft would probably need to carry close to their maximum payloads to achieve the necessary level of damage against most targets suspected of WMD activity, although any given [above-ground] structure could be destroyed with 1-3 weapons."[187] Striking Natanz, Esfahan, and Arak simultaneously would probably require 90 tactical fighters, including a 10% margin for reliability.[188] With support, this yields an Israeli strike "involving at least 100 aircraft."[189] Most sources indicate that Israel has a total of "around 350 fighter jets, a larger aerial combat force than countries of the likes of Britain and Germany."[190]

Weapons

The facilities at Esfahan and Arak are above ground, meaning they can be attacked with a variety of weaponry. Those that are underground, such as the commercial enrichment facility at Natanz, or above-ground structures that have been hardened, can be struck with precision-guided "bunker-buster" weapons, two types of which the United States has sold to Israel. The Guided Bomb Unit (GBU)-27 2000-lb class weapon carries 550 lbs of high explosives, and can penetrate more than six feet of reinforced concrete. The GBU-28 5000-lb class weapon penetrates at least 20 feet of concrete and 100 feet of earth.[191] According to CSIS, "The key weapon to be used against hard targets and underground sites like Natanz might be the GBU-28, although the US may have quietly given Israel much more sophisticated systems or Israel may have developed its own."[192]

---

[183] Scott Johnson, an analyst at IHS Jane's, in Jim Michaels, "Israeli Attack On Iran Would Be Complex," *USA Today*, February 14, 2012.

[184] Rühle, op. cit.

[185] Toukan and Cordesman, op. cit.

[186] Ibid. The IAF also has 101 F-16Is (per *Military Balance*, op. cit.).

[187] Cordesman, op. cit.

[188] Toukan and Cordesman, op. cit.

[189] Joseph Cirincione, quoted in "Expert: Attack on Iran may mean $200/barrel oil," *CBSNews.com*, February 20, 2012.

[190] Pfeffer, "Israel could strike Iran's nuclear facilities, but it won't be easy," op. cit.

[191] Toukan and Cordesman, op. cit.

[192] Cordesman, op. cit. Although small nuclear warheads, in the event Israel has them, could be effective against targets too hardened for Israel's conventional weapons to address, their use would, in the words of CSIS, "generate severe diplomatic and military consequences for Israel." Ibid.

Because the GBU-27 and -28 can be laser-guided, other aircraft or special operations forces inserted on the ground may be used to designate the target.[193]

Israel possesses Jericho II medium-range ballistic missiles with ranges capable of striking Iran.[194] They could be used against above-ground targets and free up aircraft to focus on hardened targets or those less amenable to missile attack. However, whether these ballistic missiles have the accuracy and capacity to destroy such targets in Iran is unclear.

From a weaponeering perspective, Fordow offers a unique challenge. Because the facility is reportedly built inside a mountain an estimated 295 feet deep,[195] Israel's current earth-penetrating munitions may be ineffective.[196] Observers suggest strikes against the reinforced entrance doors may be necessary, which would require a great degree of precision. Such an attack would not be possible with missiles, as the angle of approach required would not be possible from a ballistic trajectory. According to CSIS, "The hard target bombs [Israel] has acquired from the US are bunker-busters, however, not systems designed to kill underground facilities. They could damage entrances but not the facilities. What is not known is whether Israel has its own ordnance or has secretly acquired more sophisticated systems."[197]

However, it may not be necessary to damage a facility directly in order to disrupt its functionality. Centrifuges, for example, require an enormous degree of precision to work, and even a relatively minor shock or other event can destroy a centrifuge's utility. In the case of Natanz, even if the reinforced building is not breached, an explosion strong enough to significantly damage the walls could still ruin centrifuges—and the consensus of planners is that one to two GBU-28s would be sufficient to shatter the reinforced dome.[198] At Fordow, assuming that munitions would not be able to penetrate the mountainous terrain over the facility, the question would be how well the centrifuges have been isolated from shock and the possible blast effects of an attack on the facility's entrances.[199] In a *Washington Post* interview apparently contemplating a hypothetical U.S. strike on Fordow, a U.S. defense analyst was cited as a source for the following statement: "'There are good outcomes short of destroying' the centrifuge hall. Strikes against more accessible targets—from tunnel entrances and air shafts to power and water systems—can effectively knock the plant out of action."[200]

See **Figure 3** below for a graphic with reported details on the underground facilities at Natanz and Fordow and on penetrating munitions that could be used to target the facilities.

---

[193] Rühle, op. cit., states that Israel used special operations forces to designate targets in the strike on Syria's nuclear facility in 2007.

[194] Toukan and Cordesman, op. cit.

[195] Lindeman and Webster, op. cit.

[196] A former RAND Corporation analyst has argued, however, that a highly coordinated and precise attack using GBU-27s and GBU-28s could conceivably incapacitate Fordow's centrifuges. Austin Long, "Can They?", *Tablet*, November 8, 2011.

[197] Cordesman, op. cit.

[198] Rühle and Toukan/Cordesman evaluate the use of GBU-28s against Natanz; Long dedicates all GBU-28 strikes to Fordow, but finds GBU-27s sufficient for Natanz.

[199] Long, op. cit.

[200] Anthony Cordesman of CSIS cited in Warrick, "Underground sites vulnerable, experts say," op. cit.

Figure 3. Underground Nuclear Facilities and Penetrating Munitions

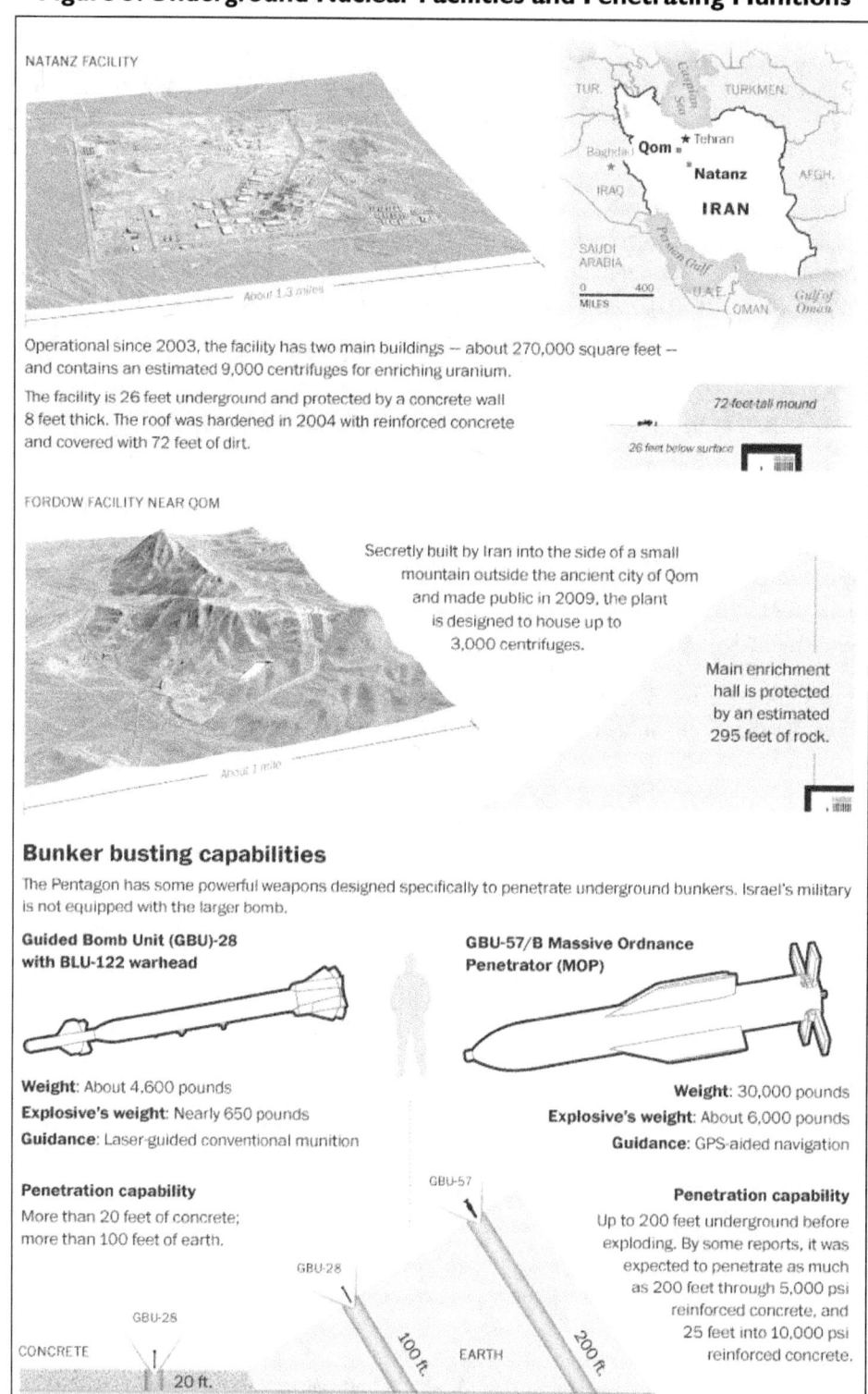

Sources: *Washington Post* (from DigitalGlobe via Google Earth Pro, GlobalSecurity.org), adapted by CRS

Note: CRS does not claim to confirm this information independently.

In a February 2012 Bipartisan Policy Center report, former Senator Charles S. Robb and retired Air Force General Charles Wald suggested that the United States provide Israel with 200 GBU-31 bunker-busting munitions and additional aerial refueling assets.[201] GBU-31s have the same warhead as Israel's existing GBU-28s (the BLU-122), but with a more precise guidance kit. Although its warhead would cause little to no more damage than a GBU-28's, the report asserts that "The GBU-31 would augment the IAF's existing capabilities, in this case by increasing the likelihood that any given sortie would score a direct hit on its target."[202] Reports indicate that Prime Minister Netanyahu might have requested additional GBU-28s and tanker aircraft from U.S. officials during his early March 2012 Washington, DC, trip, though White House Press Secretary Jay Carney claimed that the topic was not discussed in Netanyahu's meeting with the President.[203]

Potential Factors in an Israeli Decision: Estimated Effects of a Possible Strike

Effect on Iran's Nuclear Program[204]

Another major consideration for Israeli decisionmakers is the ultimate impact of an Israeli military strike on Iran's existing nuclear program. Israeli officials and analysts generally agree that a strike would not completely destroy the program. One journalist has said, "According to the Israeli assessment, a successful strike, a strike that would be conducted according to planning, would ... inflict a significant damage that would end with a delay of three to five years."[205] In February 2012, a senior Israeli official was cited in *Time* magazine as saying that "given the wide geographic dispersion of Iran's atomic facilities, combined with the limits of Israel's air armada, the Jewish state can expect to push back the Iranian program by only a matter of months—a year at most, according to the official. He attributes that estimate to the Israel Atomic Energy Commission, which is charged with assessing the likely effect of a strike."[206] In March 2012, however, another source cited optimism among some Israeli national security officials that a strike in "the next six months—conducted before Iran can further harden its nuclear sites, or make them redundant—will set back the ayatollahs' atomic ambitions at least five years."[207] Aside from

---

[201] Senator Charles S. Robb and General (USAF ret.) Charles Wald, Co-Chairs, *Meeting the Challenge: Stopping the Clock*, Bipartisan Policy Center, Washington, DC, February 2012. They make these suggestions under the following rationale: "While we do not advocate an Israeli military strike, we believe a more credible Israeli threat can only increase the pressure on Iran to negotiate." Ibid.

[202] Robb and Wald, op. cit.

[203] Kent Klein, "White House Denies Report of Deal With Israel Over Iran," *Voice of America*, March 8, 2012. According to *Reuters*, a report in Israel's *Ma'ariv* newspaper that President Obama agreed to provide the equipment on the condition that Israel not attack in 2012 was dismissed in Israeli government circles as "unrealistic." "Iran-Konflikt - Israel fordert in USA bunkerbrechende Bomben an (Israel requests bunker-buster bombs in USA)," *Reuters Deutschland*, March 8, 2012 (CRS translation).

[204] Prepared by Jim Zanotti, Specialist in Middle Eastern Affairs, with contributions from Paul K. Kerr, Analyst in Nonproliferation.

[205] Ronen Bergman, quoted in Lourdes Garcia-Navarro, "In Israel, A Nonstop Debate on Possible Iran Strike," NPR, January 31, 2012.

[206] Vick, op. cit.

[207] Jeffrey Goldberg, "Israelis Grow Confident Strike on Iran's Nukes Can Work," *Bloomberg*, March 19, 2012.

---

estimates of how much time the Iranian program might be set back as a result of a strike, Israeli officials and analysts have generally not focused in open sources on technical details that might provide hints about potential Israeli attack plans and how they might factor into Israeli decisionmaking. According to one Israeli analysis from January 2012:

> the censor's office is charged with preventing publication of secrets that may harm state security…. A public discussion ought not to deal with the operational issues connected to a military action, lest operational plans, Iranian vulnerabilities, and limitations of Israeli capabilities are exposed. In addition, the public does not have the necessary information for a discussion of this sort, such as detailed intelligence on the Iranian nuclear program and information on the IDF's operational capabilities that are relevant to such an action.[208]

Public discussion of this issue in the United States may give some hint as to the considerations Israeli leaders are addressing. Many officials and analysts in the United States have argued that, following a military attack that destroyed most of Iran's major nuclear facilities, Iran would be able to reconstitute the program.[209] General Martin Dempsey, Chairman of the Joint Chiefs of Staff, in his February 19 CNN interview, said:

> I think that Israel has the capability to strike Iran and to delay the production or the capability of Iran to achieve a nuclear weapons status, probably for a couple of years. But some of the targets are probably beyond their reach and, of course, that's what—that's what concerns them. That's this notion of a zone of immunity that they discuss.[210]

According to a February 13, 2012, CRS telephone interview with a U.S. executive branch official, an attack that left Iran's conversion and centrifuge production facilities intact would considerably reduce the timeline for reconstitution. This timeline would possibly also be affected by variables such as the number of centrifuges and quantity of LEU and 20%-enriched uranium remaining usable after an attack. Director of National Intelligence Clapper, in February 16, 2012, testimony before the Senate Armed Services Committee, said that the intelligence community does not have a "single number" for the amount of time necessary for Iran to reconstitute its program, explaining that the number of relevant variables precludes formulating such an assessment. Reconstitution of a program aimed at developing a full nuclear weapons capability would depend not only on Iran's ability to produce fissile nuclear material for a weapon, but also research, development, and production relating to the creation of both functional warheads and delivery systems such as missiles.

---

[208] Stein, et al., "The Public Discussion of Israel's Strategy Regarding a Nuclear Iran," op. cit.

[209] Kahl, "Not Time to Attack Iran…," op. cit. See also Vick, op. cit.

[210] General Dempsey transcript, op. cit.

Other Facilities Related to Iran's Nuclear Program[211]

Iran's facilities for producing centrifuges and components would probably be important to Tehran's ability to reconstitute its nuclear program after a military attack. Iran might have facilities that are unknown to Israel. IAEA inspectors had access to Iranian centrifuge workshops in order to verify an October 2003 agreement under which Iran suspended its enrichment program. However, the agency's knowledge of Iran's workshops has deteriorated since Iran ended this access in early 2006. Several months later, Wayne White, a former top Middle East intelligence analyst at the Department of State, expressed concern that Tehran could be moving some components related to its nuclear program.[212]

More recently, a U.S. official told CRS in an April 2011 in-person interview that there "could be lots of workshops" in Iran. A former U.S. government official with direct experience on the issue told CRS via telephone on February 27, 2012, that Iran's centrifuge production is widely distributed and that the number of workshops has probably multiplied "many times" since 2005 because of an increase in Iranian contractors and subcontractors working on the program. Perhaps referring to Iranian centrifuge workshops, former Central Intelligence Agency and National Security Agency Director Michael Hayden stated in January 2012 that neither the United States nor Israel knows the location of all key Iranian nuclear-related facilities.[213]

An executive branch official said in a February 27, 2012, CRS telephone interview that Iran does not have sufficient spare centrifuges or components that would enable it to install new centrifuges immediately after an attack. However, the former official interviewed on February 27 added that most centrifuge workshops could probably be rebuilt or replicated within six months.

Perhaps anticipating that a military strike might not permanently set back Iran's nuclear program, some Israeli officials reportedly acknowledge that Israel may feel compelled to mount periodic follow-up attacks[214] that, in the words of one U.S. analyst, could seek to "demoralize the industry's workforce, disrupt its operations, and greatly increase the costs of the program. Israeli leaders might hope that their attrition tactics, delivered through occasional air strikes, would bog down the nuclear program while international sanctions weaken the civilian economy and reduce political support for the regime."[215] Amos Yadlin, the former head of Israel's military intelligence unit and one of the IAF pilots who carried out the 1981 Osirak strike, wrote in March 2012 that Iran might not fully resume its nuclear program if "military action is followed by tough sanctions, stricter international inspections and an embargo on the sale of nuclear components to Tehran."[216] In contrast, a Israeli analyst wrote in January 2012, "If Israel attacks Iran now, does that mean Iran would never get nuclear weapons? No, it would merely postpone that outcome for at most a year or two more than it would take otherwise. And then it would ensure an all-out, endless bloody war thereafter."[217] Former IAF commander Eitan Ben-Eliyahu, who flew in escort of the 1981 Osirak bombing mission, was cited by the *Jerusalem Report* in March 2012 as having the view that "the ultimate success of any military operation in Iran—no matter who carries it out—will depend to a large extent on the follow-up diplomatic activity."[218]

---

[211] Prepared by Paul K. Kerr, Analyst in Nonproliferation.

[212] Paul Kerr, "News Analysis: IAEA Limits Leave Iran Intel Gaps," *Arms Control Today*, October 2006.

[213] Transcript of remarks by Michael Hayden, Center for the National Interest, Washington, DC, January 19, 2012, available at http://www.cftni.org/Hayden%20_1.19.12.pdf.

[214] Allin and Simon, op. cit., p. 53; Pfeffer, "Will They?", op. cit.

[215] Robert Haddick, "The Ticking Clock," *foreignpolicy.com*, February 10, 2012.

[216] Amos Yadlin, "Israel's Last Chance to Strike Iran," *New York Times*, February 29, 2012.

[217] Rubin, op. cit.

[218] Susser, op. cit.

Effect on Iran's Regime[219]

How the Israelis assess the effect of an air strike on the popularity and durability of Iran's regime is unclear, as is whether this is even a major factor in their decisionmaking process. In U.S.-Israel government discussions, U.S. officials reportedly have cited analyses indicating that military action against Iran's nuclear program—particularly if carried out by Israel—might heal increasingly evident rifts within Iranian society and government. U.S. officials assess that divisions are widening among Iranian elites and that Iran's economy is "weighed down by international sanctions," but they are apparently not convinced that these divisions jeopardize the regime.[220] Nevertheless, trends observed over several years—and heightened by a broad uprising in Iran in 2009 over the results of June 12, 2009, presidential elections—suggest that the regime's grip on power might be weakening. U.S. policymakers apparently do not want U.S. allies to undertake any policies that might undermine the perceived deterioration in the regime's position. Secretary of Defense Panetta, at a December 2, 2011, Brookings Institution event, stated that one of the unintended consequences of a military strike on Iran's nuclear program would be that "the regime that is weak now ... would suddenly be able to reestablish itself, suddenly be able to get support in the region."[221] That view is shared by some Iranian opposition figures, including a U.S.-based opposition figure who visited Israel in January 2012 and expressed on Israeli television the view that an Israeli air strike on Iran would increase the regime's domestic popularity.[222]

Although Israeli leaders do not generally speak publicly about the potential effect of an Israeli strike on the Iranian regime, Prime Minister Netanyahu reportedly "has told visitors [to his office] that he believes the Tehran government to be deeply unpopular, indeed despised, and that a careful attack on its nuclear facilities might even be welcomed by Iranian citizens."[223] Even if the current Iranian regime were to fall, there is no guarantee that a successor regime would be less disposed to pursuing a program that could give Iran a nuclear weapons capability. Therefore, Israeli leaders may not be particularly concerned about incurring the cost of preserving an Iranian regime that might otherwise have collapsed were there no strike. However, according to Israeli analysts who have summarized the Israeli debate over a possible military strike on Iran, regime change "is regarded by some opponents of a strike as possible, given the degree of discontent prevailing in Iran, especially among its large minorities—and as the only long-term way of rendering Iran's nuclear program less dangerous."[224]

---

[219] Prepared by Kenneth Katzman, Specialist in Middle Eastern Affairs.

[220] Testimony of Director of National Intelligence James Clapper before the Senate Select Committee on Intelligence, January 31, 2012.

[221] Transcript of Panetta's remarks at the Brookings event available at http://www.defense.gov/transcripts/transcript.aspx?transcriptid=4937.

[222] Joshua Mitnick, "Israeli defense minister implies a strike on Iran nuclear program is near," *Christian Science Monitor*, February 3, 2012. See also http://www.youtube.com/watch?v=NNWDhpOPYIY.

[223] Bronner, "Israel Senses Bluffing in Iran's Threats of Retaliation," op. cit.

[224] Feldman, et al., "What to Do About Nuclearizing Iran? The Israeli Debate," op. cit.

Potential Factors in an Israeli Decision: Possible Iranian Responses to a Strike[225]

On February 4, 2012, amid widespread reports about Israeli contemplation of a strike, Iranian Supreme Leader Khamene'i was quoted as saying that Iran will "carry out its own threat in response to the threats of war and oil sanctions should the need arise."[226] The potential consequences of a strike on Iran's nuclear program—for Israel, Israel's allies, particularly the United States, and others—are widely assessed to factor significantly into Israel's decisionmaking about a strike. Israeli open source reporting generally avoids addressing detailed Iranian response scenarios and how they might factor into Israeli decisionmaking, perhaps partly due to a belief expressed in January 2012 by three Israeli commentators (including two former officials) who have been cited earlier that "the operative capabilities [for Israel] to cope with [Iranian] responses are not a subject for public discussion because of the risks of exposure."[227] However, as discussed below, Israeli leaders such as Defense Minister Barak and public opinion polls make general references to Israel's ability to withstand a retaliation.

Beyond an Iranian response directly against Israel, Iran could choose other courses as well. At the December 2011 Brookings Institution event, Secretary Panetta raised concerns about the possible unintended consequences of a potential attack for the United States, the Middle East, and the global economy:

> the United States would obviously be blamed and we could possibly be the target of retaliation from Iran, striking our ships, striking our military bases…. [T]here are economic consequences to that attack—severe economic consequences that could impact a very fragile economy in Europe and a fragile economy here in the United States…. And lastly I think that the consequence could be that we would have an escalation that would take place that would not only involve many lives, but I think could consume the Middle East in a confrontation and a conflict that we would regret.[228]

Although some of Iran's threatened responses are specific—such as its as-yet unimplemented December 2011 threat to close the Strait of Hormuz if sanctions were placed on Iran's Central Bank—most are vague. The potential Iranian responses discussed below are intended to be suggestive, not exhaustive or definitive. For purposes of clarity, they are discussed in terms of increasing degrees of severity. It is also possible that Iran would pursue multiple responses simultaneously, or not respond at all.

Diplomatic Responses

It is possible that Iran might respond to an Israeli strike not with military action, but with a diplomatic reaction intended to attract international sympathy, reduce its isolation, and perhaps even ease international and multilateral sanctions. Iran could take advantage of pre-existing international criticism of Israel on the Palestinian question and other issues to portray itself as a

---

[225] Prepared by Kenneth Katzman, Specialist in Middle Eastern Affairs, except as otherwise specified.

[226] "Iran will carry out its threats if necessary: Leader," *Mehr News Agency*, February 3, 2012.

[227] Stein, et al., "The Public Discussion of Israel's Strategy Regarding a Nuclear Iran," op. cit.

[228] Panetta Brookings transcript, op. cit.

victim of "unwarranted and unprovoked Israeli aggression" that Iran might argue violated international law.

Under this scenario, Iran still might not be able to persuade the U.N. Security Council to lift existing U.N. sanctions. However, the continued effectiveness of many international and multilateral sanctions against Iran would depend on the degree of international compliance and enforcement. Iran could possibly use the Israeli strike to convince countries opposed to the strike or skeptical of the overall utility of sanctions to abandon their adherence to the sanctions regime. Additional international sanctions or international compliance with existing U.S. and EU sanctions might become very difficult to obtain or maintain.[229]

Hostile but Non-Military Responses

Another option for Iran could be considered hostile to the international community, but would not involve military action. In the aftermath of an Israeli air strike, Iran could try to reconstitute its nuclear program rather than accept a permanent setback. Presumably, Iran would do so in sites that are hardened and well defended to try to deter another such strike.[230]

As part of such an effort, Iran could possibly stop permitting the IAEA to monitor Iran's compliance with its Safeguards Agreement. Iran could cease allowing IAEA visits, stop responding to IAEA questions, and/or withdraw from the NPT outright.[231] Anticipation of these measures could influence Israeli decisionmaking regarding a strike because an end to IAEA monitoring would deprive the international community of valuable sources of first-hand information on Iran's nuclear program. An NPT withdrawal could also undermine the international legal basis for action to prevent Iran from acquiring a nuclear weapons capability.

Military Responses

One major question for Israeli leaders to consider is whether Iran, were it to respond militarily or otherwise violently to an Israeli air strike, would confine its response to Israel-related targets or expand its response to the United States and other countries deemed complicit. On February 14, 2012, the head of the Iranian Revolutionary Guard Corps (IRGC) Public Relations Department said Israel would face "appalling retaliation" for an attack on Iran, and that any military strike will have "terrible and inconceivable consequences" for the United States and its allies.[232] In mid March, Supreme Leader Khamene'i was quoted as saying on Iranian state television that "against an attack by enemies—to defend ourselves either against the U.S. or Zionist regime—we will attack them on the same level that they attack us."[233] Nevertheless, the breadth of Iranian retaliation might depend on how the strike were carried out, which route(s) were used, what reported communications there were, if any, between Israel and other governments, and similar factors.

---

[229] William Maclean, "Iran raid likely to drag in U.S. and hurt global economy," *Reuters*, February 5, 2012.

[230] Vick, op. cit.

[231] Maclean, op. cit.

[232] "Israel War on Iran Will Evoke Gory Retaliation: Commander," Iran Press TV, February 14, 2012.

[233] "Iran vows to retaliate 'on the same level' to US or Israel attack," msnbc.com, March 21, 2012.

Attacks on Israeli Territory

Israeli officials are, by almost all accounts, braced for an Iranian response on Israeli territory, were there to be a strike against Iran. The forms of Iranian response could determine whether Iran's responses set off a regional war involving other states, or remain relatively confined to attacks that Israel could absorb or against which it would counter-attack with its own capabilities. According to one Israeli report:

> If it comes to a shooting war, Israel will face an estimated 200,000 rockets and missiles in enemy hands in Iran, Syria, Lebanon and Gaza. According to Military Intelligence Chief Aviv Kochavi, most have a range of up to 40 kilometers (25 miles), and there are a few thousand with ranges of between 100 and 1,300 kilometers (60-800 miles). All of northern and central Israel is within range of Lebanon, Syria and Iran while rockets from Gaza threaten most of the south.[234]

In previous instances—1991 during the Gulf War, 2006 against Hezbollah, 2008-2009 against Hamas and other Palestinian militants—Israelis took cover in bomb shelters and safe rooms. According to reports, approximately 50 Israeli civilians were directly killed by missile and rocket strikes during these three conflicts combined.[235] But there are concerns that retaliatory missile attacks by Iran could be of an altogether different magnitude. In addition, some Israeli reports have raised concerns regarding the level of Israel's civil defense preparedness. According to one, "1.7 million Israelis, a quarter of the population, do not have ready access to bomb shelters. An estimated $256 million is needed to produce gas masks for the 40 percent of Israelis who do not have them."[236] A late February 2012 poll indicated that by a 60%-25% margin, a majority of Israelis disagree with Defense Minister Barak's statement that in case of an attack on Iran, if Israeli citizens obey instructions and remain in their homes, Iran's retaliatory strikes will probably cause only about 500 casualties. The poll indicated that the majority believed that the number of casualties would be higher.[237] A March 2012 poll indicated, however, that 65% of Jewish Israelis believe that "the price Israel would have to pay for living under the shadow of the Iranian nuclear bomb is higher than the price it would pay for attacking Iran's nuclear capability."[238]

---

[234] Susser, op. cit.

[235] Greenberg, "Sense of inevitable war grips Israel," op. cit. According to information provided by Israel's embassy in Washington, DC on March 8, 2012, the *Jerusalem Post* reported on January 7, 1992 that 72 Israeli civilians died indirectly from but as a consequence of Iraqi Scud missile attacks during the 1991 Gulf War—four from gas mask suffocation and 68 from heart attacks. Thousands of Israeli civilians were injured in the previous three conflicts combined, and the casualty numbers do not fully measure psychological effects. The combined cost in the three conflicts of property damage, civil defense and military preparedness (including evacuation and relocation of civilians), and the inability of many Israelis to work under emergency conditions is estimated to be in the billions.

[236] Susser, op. cit. See also Eiran, op. cit.

[237] Dahaf Institute poll, February 28-29, 2012, with a 4.5% margin of error, details available at http://www.peaceindex.org/indexMonthEng.aspx?num=240#anchor269.

[238] Poll conducted by Professor Camil Fuchs of Tel Aviv University for the Jerusalem Center for Public Affairs. Details of the poll, whose margin of error is unspecified, available at http://jcpa.org/JCPA/Templates/ShowPage.asp?DBID=1&LNGID=1&TMID=111&FID=254&PID=0&IID=13295.

Iranian Ballistic Missile Attacks[239]

It is clear from the many reports discussing the possibility of an Israeli air strike that Israeli leaders generally assume that, at the very least, Iran would retaliate against Israel directly with ballistic missiles.[240] According to one U.S. defense analyst, this could include "Israeli military and civilian centers, and Israeli suspected nuclear weapons sites."[241] Iranian leaders almost certainly calculate that missile strikes against Israel could provoke additional escalation and— perhaps more importantly—bring the United States into conflict with Iran, whether or not Iran conducted any strikes against U.S. targets.[242] Still, Iranian leaders could be under significant pressure from key constituencies, such as the IRGC, to demonstrate a forthright response to an Israeli strike. It is widely expected that Israel would prepare and deploy its ballistic missile defense capabilities prior to attacking Iran.

Although Iran has perhaps the largest inventory of ballistic missiles in the Middle East, Iran cannot reach targets in Israel with its hundreds of short-range ballistic missiles (SRBMs) because of the distances involved. However, Iran reportedly has a number of medium-range ballistic missiles (MRBMs) that could strike anywhere within Israel. This includes the liquid-fueled Shahab-3 and its variants, whose range estimates in open sources vary from 1,000 kilometers to almost 2,000 kilometers. Exact numbers are not publicly known, but estimates are that Iran has less than 50 Shahab-3 launchers (for all its variant missiles) and perhaps 25-100+ Shahab-3 missiles (including variant versions).[243] In recent years, Iran also has developed and tested solid-fueled Sejil-1 and Sejil-2 MRBMs with ranges estimated upwards of 2,000 kilometers or greater. **Figure 4** below illustrates potential ranges of these MRBMs.

---

[239] Prepared by Steven A. Hildreth, Specialist in Missile Defense; and Kenneth Katzman, Specialist in Middle Eastern Affairs.

[240] See, e.g., Bergman, "Will Israel Attack Iran?", op. cit.

[241] Cordesman, op. cit.

[242] A U.S. national security columnist has written, "Administration officials caution that Tehran shouldn't misunderstand: The United States has a 60-year commitment to Israeli security, and if Israel's population centers were hit, the United States could feel obligated to come to Israel's defense." Ignatius, op. cit.

[243] Various. See, e.g., "Iran's Ballistic Missile Capabilities: A Net Assessment," Michael Elleman, International Institute for Strategic Studies, May 2010, p. 20; "Ballistic and Cruise Missile Threat," National Air and Space Intelligence Center, NASIC-10301-0985-09, Wright-Patterson Air Force Base, 2009, p. 17.

Figure 4. Potential Ranges of Iranian Medium-Range Ballistic Missiles

(calculated from possible launch sites)

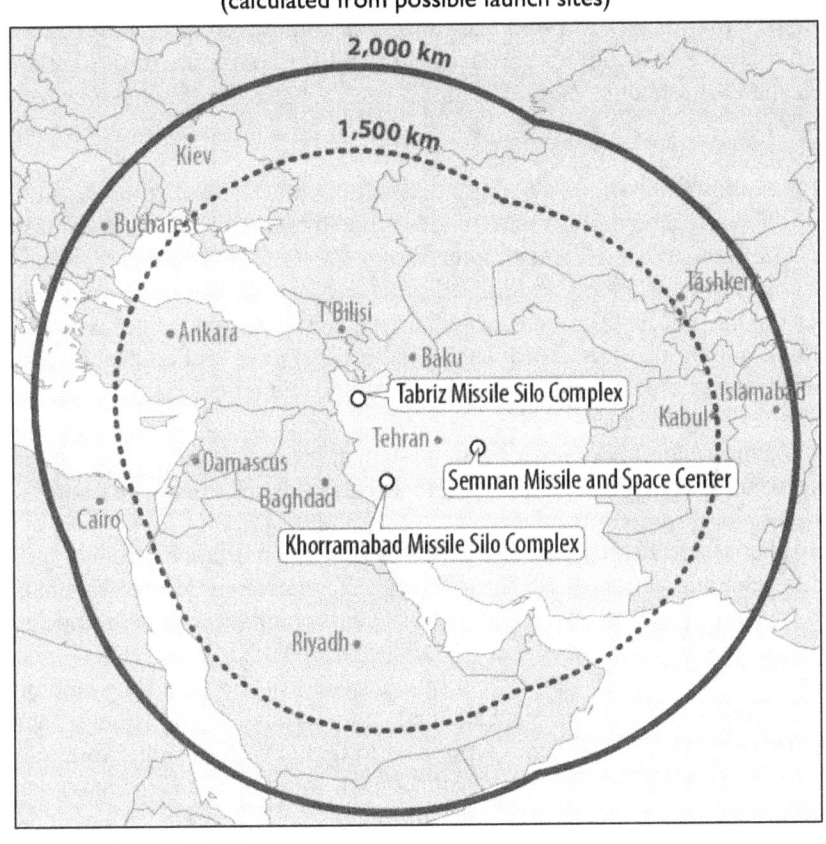

Sources: Various, adapted by CRS.

Notes: All ranges are approximate.

It is very difficult to project the number of potential Israeli casualties from an Iranian ballistic missile counter-attack against Israel. Because of the conventional yields and relative inaccuracies of the Iranian missiles, a relatively low Israeli casualty count might hold true. But if the ballistic missile attack is sizeable and hits large population densities in city cores, casualties could be significantly higher.

Attacks by Lebanese Hezbollah and Hamas or Other Palestinian Militants[244]

Many Israeli analysts assert that Iran would respond against Israel using allied non-state actors such as Lebanese Hezbollah.[245] Iran has reportedly supplied Hezbollah with about 50,000 missiles and rockets, including several thousand that can reportedly target Israeli population centers significantly farther south than those hit in the 2006 war—including Tel Aviv and its vicinity.[246] For possible ranges, see **Figure 5** below. However, over the past 15 years Hezbollah

---

[244] For more information, see CRS Report R41446, *Hezbollah: Background and Issues for Congress*, by Casey L. Addis and Christopher M. Blanchard; and CRS Report R41514, *Hamas: Background and Issues for Congress*, by Jim Zanotti.

[245] Bronner, "Israel Senses Bluffing in Iran's Threats of Retaliation," op. cit.

[246] Bergman, "Will Israel Attack Iran?", op. cit.

has evolved from a reflexive proxy of Iran into a political and military force in Lebanon in its own right. Hezbollah might ultimately decide independently to stay out of any retaliatory operations against Israel, in part to avoid starting a long-running conflict with Israel similar to that which occurred in 2006. Additionally, according to the *Economist*, "the situation in Syria means that [Hezbollah] cannot be certain that, if it fires at Israel, its Iranian-supplied arsenal will be replenished."[247]

Iran has always had far less influence over the Palestinian Sunni Islamist movement Hamas, which controls the Gaza Strip and is routinely described by Israeli officials as an Iranian proxy. Ongoing unrest in Syria and its violent suppression by the Asad regime has reportedly led to a weakening of ties between Hamas and Iran and to fissures within Hamas itself, as Hamas's external leadership has left its Damascus headquarters, said that "we are not with the regime in its security solution," and emphasized its Muslim Brotherhood roots.[248] Perhaps in an attempt to keep its ties with Hamas's Gaza leadership strong, Iran hosted Ismail Haniyeh, Hamas's prime minister in Gaza, in early February.[249] Reports indicate that Iran is also providing more resources to Palestinian Islamic Jihad (PIJ), another Sunni Islamist group based in Gaza, possibly to maintain its influence there in the event of a further drift in its relations with Hamas.

Between them, Hamas and PIJ have thousands of rockets and mortars capable of hitting Israel—including some that could approach Tel Aviv. Though they have not demonstrated ability to carry out major non-rocket terrorist attacks within major Israeli population centers since 2006, the year Hamas became more politically active and won Palestinian Authority legislative elections, Hamas and PIJ may be capable of terrorist attacks on Israeli settlers in the West Bank and on Israelis near Gaza and the Egyptian border. Given these factors, and also considering Israel's demonstrated ability to retaliate against rocket launching militants in Gaza and the reportedly successful deployment of its Iron Dome short-range missile defense system,[250] it is unclear whether Iran can count on Hamas or PIJ to respond on Iran's behalf to an Israeli air strike. In early March 2012, some senior Hamas leaders reportedly stated that an Israeli attack on Iran alone would not cause Hamas to retaliate, and reports conflicted over whether other senior leaders disagreed with this stance.[251]

---

[247] "Attacking Iran: Up in the air," *Economist*, February 25, 2012.

[248] "Hamas 'to renounce' armed resistance to Israel," *Jane's Intelligence Weekly*, December 15, 2011; Ehud Yaari, "The agony of Hamas," *Times of Israel*, February 27, 2012; Mohammed Daraghmeh, "AP Interview: Hamas out of Syria, leader says," *Associated Press*, February 26, 2012.

[249] Fares Akram and Isabel Kershner, "Hamas Premier Visits Iran in Sign That Ties Are Strong," *New York Times*, February 11, 2012.

[250] For more information on Iron Dome, see CRS Report RL33476, *Israel: Background and U.S. Relations*, by Jim Zanotti.

[251] Harriet Sherwood, "Hamas rules out military support for Iran in any war with Israel," *guardian.co.uk*, March 6, 2012; "US arms offer to Israel to delay hit," *Agence France Presse*, March 9, 2012. "'Hamas denies it would stay out of Israel-Iran war,'" *jpost.com*, March 8, 2012.

Figure 5. Possible Ranges of Rockets and Missiles from Iranian-Allied Groups

(as of February 2012)

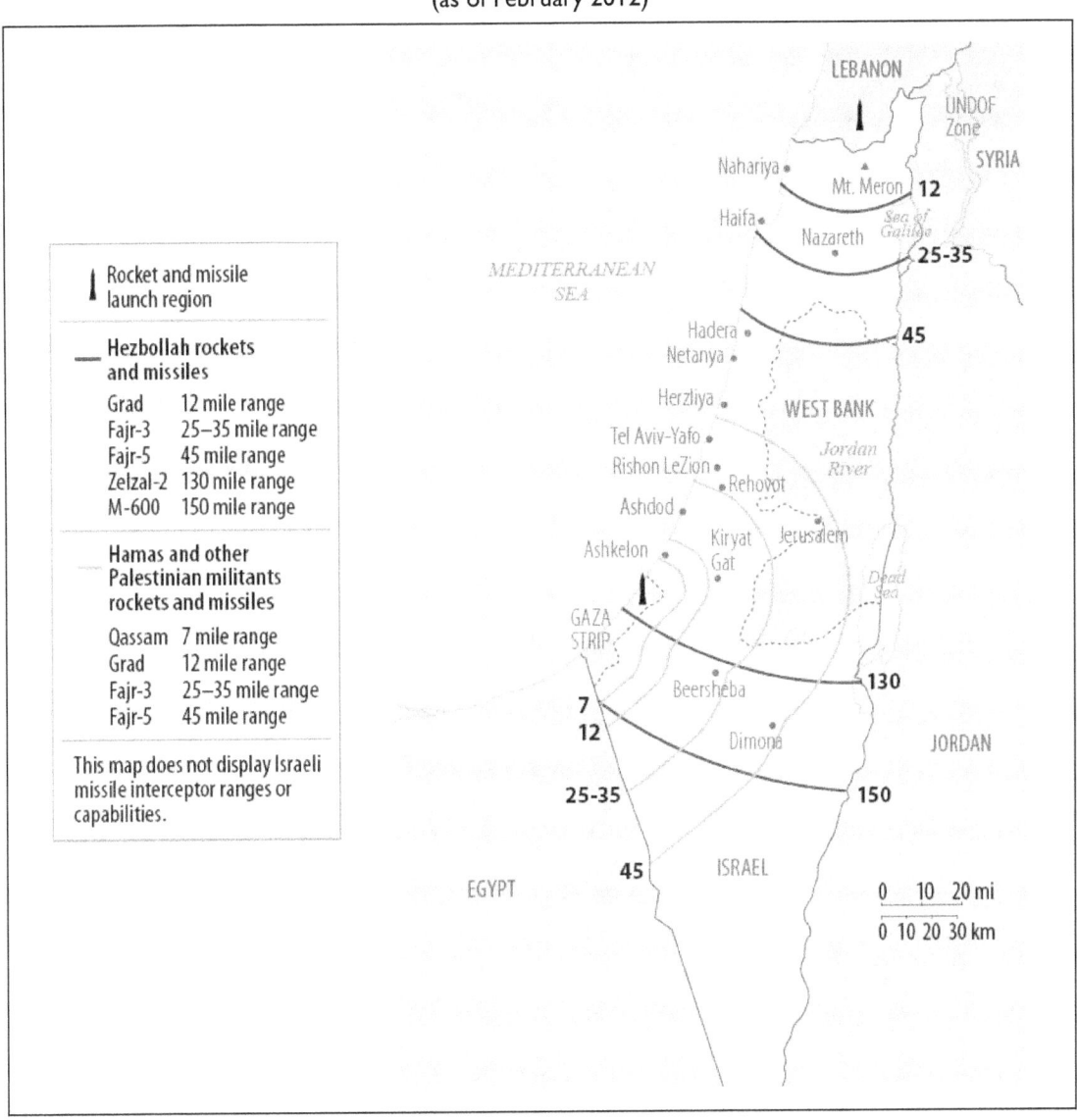

Source: Bipartisan Policy Center, adapted by CRS.

Notes: All ranges are approximate.

Possible Israeli Missile Defense Capabilities[252]

Israel has deployed ballistic missile defense (BMD) capabilities designed specifically for countering short- and medium-range ballistic attacks, as well as indigenous defenses (such as the Iron Dome system mentioned above) against possible rocket barrages. The United States contributes annually to the cooperative U.S.-Israel BMD programs known as David's Sling (for SRBMs—which is not yet deployed) and Arrow (for MRBMs), and has sold Patriot air defense

---

[252] Prepared by Steven A. Hildreth, Specialist in Missile Defense.

batteries to Israel.[253] Although Israel reports high confidence in the abilities of those BMD systems that they have deployed, Israel has not tested how well they would perform in wartime. In general, some weapon systems, including the performance of U.S. BMD systems, have not performed as well in actual combat conditions as in limited developmental or operational test environments.[254] One Israeli journalist has expressed concern about Israeli missile defense capabilities and costs in the event of retaliation by Iran and its allies to an Israeli strike:

> Israel's active missile defense systems—the Arrow, Patriot and Iron Dome (Magic Wand/David's Sling will only be operative in 2013)—will be severely tested. Besides the difficulty of dealing with multiple missile attacks, active defense is also extremely expensive. Each Arrow missile costs around $2.7 million and each Iron Dome projectile around $80,000.[255]

In addition to Israel's own capabilities, the United States has naval and other BMD capabilities in theater that could be used to support Israel's efforts to deal with an Iranian ballistic missile counter-attack, if a decision to do so were made.[256]

Attacks Against Israeli Interests Abroad

Many analysts have stated that Iran would possibly target Israeli facilities and diplomats abroad as part of its retaliatory strategy. Agents of the IRGC Qods Force, which is the arm of the IRGC that operates outside Iran's borders, regularly cooperating with Hezbollah, would presumably be involved in such retaliation. Hezbollah has been implicated in the July 1992 bombing of Israel's embassy in Buenos Aires,[257] and—along with the Qods Force—in the bombing of a Jewish cultural center (AMIA building) in that same city two years later.[258] Combined, the two bombings killed approximately 114 people and injured hundreds more.[259]

At least one Israeli journalist has pointed to events in February 2012 as an indicator that Iran might employ such an approach.[260] Attacks, attempted attacks, and alleged attack plots were conducted or revealed against Israeli diplomatic personnel in several countries, including

---

[253] For more information on U.S. cooperation with Israel on missile defense, see CRS Report RL33476, *Israel: Background and U.S. Relations*, by Jim Zanotti; and CRS Report RL33222, *U.S. Foreign Aid to Israel*, by Jeremy M. Sharp.

[254] See, e.g., House of Representatives, Performance of the Patriot Missile in the Gulf War: Hearing before the Legislation and National Security Subcommittee of the Committee on Government Operations, 102 Cong., 2nd Sess., 7 April 1992; U.S. Government Printing Office (Washington DC: 1993), and Operation Desert Storm: Evaluation of the Air War, GAO/PEMD-96-10, July 1996.

[255] Susser, op. cit.

[256] The United States and Israel have worked closely together for several years in simulated and actual war gaming exercises that focused on countering a ballistic missile attack against Israel.

[257] U.S. State Department, Country Reports on Terrorism 2010, Chapter 6. Foreign Terrorist Organizations, August 18, 2011.

[258] Ibid.; Yaakov Katz, "Iran's Quds Force expanding in Europe, S. America," *jpost.com*, January 6, 2012.

[259] These figures come from the State Department's Patterns of Global Terrorism report for 1992, available at http://www.fas.org/irp/threat/terror_92/review.html, and a July 18, 2007, item on the Israeli Foreign Ministry's website commemorating the 13th anniversary of the 1994 AMIA bombing. Iran's current Defense Minister, Ahmad Vahidi, was head of the Qods Force when the AMIA bombing was conducted, and he is wanted for questioning by Interpol for that attack. Aidan Jones, "Ahmadinejad chooses wanted man for cabinet," *guardian.co.uk*, August 22, 2009.

[260] Yaakov Katz, "Why is Iran having a hard time targeting Israeli diplomats?", *Jerusalem Post*, February 17, 2012.

Thailand, Georgia, India, and Azerbaijan.[261] Israel blamed Iran for these events, although investigators in most of the countries have not announced definitive conclusions to that effect. Israeli leaders appear to believe that Iran may be attempting copycat retaliations against Israel for a series of seemingly related assassinations of Iranian nuclear scientists over the past two years, the most recent of which occurred in January 2012.[262]

Expanded Military Responses

It is unclear how significantly contingencies of Iran potentially attacking U.S. targets in response to an Israeli strike factor into Israeli decisionmaking. Some Israeli analysts have argued that the Israeli public debate should include greater discussion of how a possible Iranian retaliation aimed at U.S. targets or interests might affect the overall risk-benefit assessment of an Israeli strike:

> The possibility that in the event of an Israeli military action Iran would decide to attack US targets in the Gulf or target oil exports cannot be ruled out. In such a case, the United States would be forced to respond, and would thus find itself involved in a military confrontation it did not initiate. This might have serious consequences on American public opinion (not to mention some of its elected officials) toward Israel, which will have involved the United States in a war.[263]

According to one report citing U.S. officials, based on the results of a March 2012 U.S. Central Command (CENTCOM) exercise simulating the repercussions of a possible Israeli attack on Iran, CENTCOM's commander General James Mattis reportedly told aides that "an Israeli first strike would be likely to have dire consequences across the region and for United States forces there."[264]

Attempted Closure of the Strait of Hormuz

One potential scenario that Israeli decisionmakers may consider, were Iran to expand its retaliation beyond Israeli targets, would be an Iranian attempt to close the Strait of Hormuz. In December 2011 and January 2012, Iran issued the threat in response to looming additional economic sanctions, not specifically in response to reports of a possible Israeli air strike. Nevertheless, the threat suggests that Iranian leaders see closing the Strait or attacking ships transiting it as a viable option for raising the cost to international actors of pressure on Iran—no matter what form that pressure might take.[265] An Israeli analysis co-authored in January 2012 by former head of military intelligence Amos Yadlin, and not explicitly contemplating Iranian responses to a possible Israeli military strike, expressed skepticism in Iran's abilities to block the Strait for an extended period and further asserted that doing so would run counter to Iran's own economic and strategic interests.[266] For more information on possible conflict scenarios in the

---

[261] Thomas Fuller and Rick Gladstone, "Explosions in Thailand Cast Suspicion on Iranians," *New York Times*, February 15, 2012. The *Jerusalem Post* has reported that similar plots may have been foiled in Bulgaria, Egypt, and Turkey as well since January 2012. Katz, op. cit.

[262] See transcript of Public Radio International's *The World* show from February 14, 2012, entitled, "Thailand Blasts: 'Iranian' Bomber Injured in Bangkok."

[263] Stein, et al., "The Public Discussion of Israel's Strategy Regarding a Nuclear Iran," op. cit.

[264] Mark Mazzetti and Thom Shanker, "U.S. Simulation Forecasts Perils of Strike at Iran," *New York Times*, March 20, 2012.

[265] See, e.g., Maclean, op. cit.

[266] Amos Yadlin and Yoel Guzansky, "The Strait of Hormuz: Assessing and Neutralizing the Threat," *Strategic* (continued...)

Strait, see CRS Report R42335, *Iran's Threat to the Strait of Hormuz*, coordinated by Kenneth Katzman.

Attacks on U.S. Allies in the Persian Gulf

Israeli decisionmakers might also be influenced by the possibility of Iranian attacks on U.S. allies in the Persian Gulf—the states of the Gulf Cooperation Council (GCC: Saudi Arabia, Kuwait, Qatar, Bahrain, the United Arab Emirates [UAE], and Oman).[267] All of these countries have formal defense or facilities access agreements with the United States, and most have had contentious or even hostile relations with Iran since its 1979 Islamic Revolution, although to varying degrees. All have been publicly critical of Iran's nuclear program, and some Saudi royal family members have implied that Saudi Arabia would seek nuclear weapons if Iran obtains them.[268] Analysts see Saudi Arabia, in particular, as a leader in efforts to weaken Iran's influence in the region. Several GCC leaders, including those of Saudi Arabia, Bahrain, and UAE, have been widely cited in press reports as supporting an air strike on Iran's nuclear program, though in the context of a possible U.S. strike, not an Israeli strike.[269] Nonetheless, Iran might not want to risk a response against the GCC that could cause its members—and with them, other Arab states—to support the Israeli action.

All of the GCC states are oil exporters and most have oil loading terminals on the Gulf that are within easy range of Iranian ballistic or cruise missiles. During the 1980-1988 Iran-Iraq war—particularly the last two years when Iran perceived the United States had entered the war on Iraq's side—Iran attacked some of the Gulf states' facilities, particularly those of Kuwait.[270] Israel does not maintain diplomatic relations with any GCC states. Although Israeli officials have not spoken publicly about the possibility of Iranian retaliation against GCC states, in addition to possible Israeli concerns that such a retaliation might cause the United States to view an Israeli strike negatively because of close U.S. security ties with GCC states, Israel might weigh the possibility that such a retaliation could further antagonize GCC governments and populations toward Israel.

Attacks on U.S. Installations and Interests in the Region or Elsewhere Abroad

Another possible concern for Israeli decisionmakers, as mentioned above in multiple quotes from Israeli commentators, is how a potential Iranian response against U.S. interests in the region might affect U.S. official and public views on a strike and U.S.-Israel relations more broadly. Secretary Panetta and others have anticipated that, were Iran to expand its response to U.S. targets, it would target U.S. personnel in Iraq and Afghanistan. The last U.S. combat troops left Iraq in December 2011, but there are still over 16,000 U.S. personnel there (diplomats, other civilian officials, security contractors, and others), including those based at the large U.S. Embassy in Baghdad and at U.S. consulates in Basra and Irbil. U.S. officials have repeatedly asserted that agents of Iran's Qods Force are present in Iraq, building influence with and providing material assistance to Iraqi factions and militias. Like Lebanese Hezbollah, these Iraqi

---

(...continued)

Assessment, vol. 14, no. 4, January 2012.

[267] Allin and Simon, op. cit., p. 101.

[268] Hugh Tomlinson, "Saudi Arabia to acquire nuclear weapons to counter Iran," *The Times* (UK), February 11, 2012.

[269] Ross Colvin, "'Cut Off the Head of the Snake,' Saudis Told U.S.," *Reuters,* November 29, 2010.

[270] CRS Report R42335, *Iran's Threat to the Strait of Hormuz,* coordinated by Kenneth Katzman.

factions have their own independent objectives in Iraqi politics and are not controlled by Tehran, but they are widely assessed to be susceptible to Iranian influence. Pro-Iranian Iraqi Shiite militias are particularly prevalent in southern Iraq, particularly Basra. Analysts perceive that Iran would have ample capability to retaliate there against U.S. personnel following an Israeli air strike.[271]

There is also the threat of a potential Iranian response in Afghanistan. Approximately 90,000 U.S. military personnel remain in Afghanistan as of March 2012, but Iran has substantially less influence in Afghanistan than it does in Iraq. Nevertheless, as with Iraq, U.S. officials and U.S. government reports consistently assert that Iran—through the Qods Force—is arming and training anti-U.S. elements in Afghanistan—in this case, anti-government Taliban militants.[272] This suggests that Iran sees potential in retaliating against the United States in Afghanistan.[273]

The Qods Force is widely believed to operate extensively in some GCC states. On occasion, some GCC countries, particularly Kuwait, have arrested purported Qods Force agents who were allegedly spying or attempting to support Shiite opposition groups in some of these states. U.S. officials accused a Qods-supported Shiite opposition group of a lead role in the June 1996 bombing of the Khobar Towers housing complex, in which 19 U.S. Air Force officers were killed. Other U.S. targets in GCC states that Iran might try to attack include the numerous military bases and other facilities that the U.S. military accesses, U.S. embassies, and offices of U.S.-based multinational corporations. The latter are particularly prevalent in the UAE emirate of Dubai. Additionally, according to *Bloomberg*, Ali Hajizadeh, commander of the air defense division of the IRGC, said in November 2011 that a newly deployed U.S. X-Band radar in eastern Turkey that is part of a NATO-approved missile defense system for Europe would be a target for Iran "if there is a threat."[274]

Some believe that Iran, using the Qods Force, could try to retaliate against U.S. targets outside the Middle East—for example in Europe, Asia, Latin America, or elsewhere. U.S. officials have asserted that the Qods Force has a presence in Venezuela, for example,[275] and the force is known to operate worldwide.

Possible Attacks on the U.S. Homeland

At least one reported Israeli source, along with some U.S. officials and outside analysts, has suggested or implied that Iran could have the capability to retaliate inside the United States itself if there were an Israeli strike against Iran. An internal Israeli security document that ABC News claimed it obtained in early February 2012 reportedly indicated concern that sites in North America—including both Israeli government sites (embassies and consulates) and Jewish religious and cultural sites (synagogues, schools, community centers) were subject to an increased threat from Iran.[276] Law enforcement officials have reportedly stepped up patrols around Jewish

---

[271] CRS Report RS21968, *Iraq: Politics, Governance, and Human Rights*, by Kenneth Katzman.

[272] State Department Country Reports on Terrorism 2010, Chapter 3: State Sponsors of Terrorism, "Iran."

[273] For more information on Iran's influence in Afghanistan, see: CRS Report RL32048, *Iran: U.S. Concerns and Policy Responses*, by Kenneth Katzman.

[274] Emre Peker, "Iran-Turkey Ties Under Increasing Strain From Mideast Sunni-Shiite Divide," *Bloomberg*, February 2, 2012.

[275] Department of Defense, "Unclassified Report on Military Power of Iran," April 2010.

[276] Richard Esposito, "Exclusive: Israel Warns US Jews: Iran Could Strike Here," ABC News, February 3, 2012.

sites in some major U.S. urban areas.[277] Assessments of possible Iranian infiltration of the U.S. homeland are based in part on an alleged plot—contained in a Justice Department indictment filed in October 2011—that an Iranian-American citizen working with officials in the Qods Force sought to kill the Saudi Ambassador in Washington, DC. Citing the alleged plot, Director of National Intelligence James Clapper testified on January 31, 2012, before the Senate Select Intelligence Committee that:

> The 2011 plot to assassinate the Saudi Ambassador to the United States shows that some Iranian officials—probably including Supreme Leader Ali Khamene'i—have changed their calculus and are now more willing to conduct an attack in the United States in response to real or perceived U.S. actions that threaten the regime.

U.S. officials have incorporated into their assessments Tehran's calculations about the risks of taking such a step. Director Clapper, in his testimony, added that "Iran's willingness to sponsor future attacks in the United States ... probably will be shaped by Tehran's evaluation of the costs it bears." It is unclear how much these considerations factor into Israeli assessments of the possible consequences of a strike.

Conclusion: Possible Implications for Congress[278]

According to one assessment by two U.S. analysts:

> an Israeli decision to risk indeterminate war with the Islamic Republic ... would be momentous, transforming the regional order in ways that cannot be inferred from past wars.[279]

This report discusses many factors that may influence the Israeli debate and a possible decision by its leaders regarding military action against Iranian nuclear facilities.

An Israeli strike on Iran could raise significant questions for Members of Congress, both short- and long-term. These include, but are not limited to, the following:

- How might a strike affect options and debate regarding short-term and long-term U.S. relations and security cooperation with, and foreign assistance to, Israel and other regional countries?[280]

---

[277] Ibid.; Mitchell D. Silber, "The Iranian Threat to New York City," *Wall Street Journal*, February 14, 2012; "Tensions with Iran raise US safety concerns, but intelligence official says attack unlikely," *Associated Press*, February 17, 2012.

[278] Prepared by Jim Zanotti, Specialist in Middle Eastern Affairs.

[279] Allin and Simon, op. cit., p. 105.

[280] On March 5, 2012, House Majority Leader Eric Cantor introduced the United States-Israel Enhanced Security Cooperation Act of 2012 (H.R. 4133). The bill, if enacted, would require the President to report on the status of Israel's "qualitative military edge" within 180 days, while also expressing the sense of Congress that the United States should take the following actions, among others, in support of Israel: (1) Provide Israel such support as may be necessary to increase development and production of joint missile defense systems, particularly such systems that defend the urgent threat posed to Israel and United States forces in the region; (2) Provide Israel defense articles and defense services through such mechanisms as appropriate, to include air refueling tankers, missile defense capabilities, and specialized munitions; (3) Allocate additional weaponry and munitions for the forward-deployed United States stockpile in Israel; (4) Provide Israel additional surplus defense articles and defense services, as appropriate, in the wake of the withdrawal of United States forces from Iraq. The bill has been referred to the House Foreign Affairs Committee. Senator Barbara (continued...)

- Would an Israeli strike on Iranian nuclear facilities be considered self-defense? Why or why not? What would be the legal and policy implications either way?[281]

- How might a strike affect the implementation of existing sanctions legislation on Iran or options and debate over new legislation on the subject?[282]

- How might Congress consult with the Obama Administration on and provide oversight with respect to various political and military options?

Author Contact Information

Jim Zanotti, Coordinator
Specialist in Middle Eastern Affairs
jzanotti@crs.loc.gov, 7-1441

Kenneth Katzman
Specialist in Middle Eastern Affairs
kkatzman@crs.loc.gov, 7-7612

Jeremiah Gertler
Specialist in Military Aviation
jgertler@crs.loc.gov, 7-5107

Steven A. Hildreth
Specialist in Missile Defense
shildreth@crs.loc.gov, 7-7635

Acknowledgments

Amber Hope Wilhelm provided and adapted graphics for this report.

(...continued)

Boxer introduced a slightly different version of this bill (S. 2165) on March 6, 2012. Reports in late March 2012 indicate that the Department of Defense intends to ask Congress for additional funding to Israel—perhaps more than $500 million—for up to 10 additional Iron Dome short-range missile defense batteries. Barbara Opall-Rome and Marcus Weisberger, "Pentagon Plans Major Funding Boost for Israel's Iron Dome," *Defense News*, March 27, 2012. Congressman Howard Berman had introduced the Iron Dome Support Act (H.R. 4229) on March 21, 2012.

[281] See footnote 158. The July 23, 1952 Mutual Defense Assistance Agreement between the United States and Israel (TIAS 2675) states, "The Government of Israel assures the United States Government that such equipment, materials, or services as may be acquired from the United States ... are required for and will be used solely to maintain its internal security, its legitimate self-defense ... and that it will not undertake any act of aggression against any other state." Section 4 of the Arms Export Control Act of 1976 (AECA, P.L. 94-329) contains a similar requirement that arms supplied by the United States to other countries be used solely for purposes of self-defense. Section 3(c)(2) of the AECA requires the President to report promptly to the Congress upon the receipt of information that a "substantial violation" described in section 3(c)(1) of the AECA "may have occurred" pertaining to the possible breach of an existing agreement or of section 4. For more information on this requirement and the Reagan Administration's actions pursuant to the AECA following Israel's 1981 attack on Iraq's Osirak reactor, see CRS Report R42385, *U.S. Defense Articles and Services Supplied to Foreign Recipients: Restrictions on Their Use*, by Richard F. Grimmett.

[282] Bills in the 112th Congress that, if enacted, would expand sanctions or seek to promote their implementation include the Iran Sanctions, Accountability, and Human Rights Act of 2012 (S. 2101), reported out of the Senate Banking, Housing, and Urban Affairs Committee on February 13, 2012; and the Iran Threat Reduction Act of 2011 (H.R. 1905), which was passed by the House by a 410-11 vote on December 14, 2011, and referred to the Senate Foreign Relations Committee. See CRS Report RS20871, *Iran Sanctions*, by Kenneth Katzman.

www.ingramcontent.com/pod-product-compliance
Lightning Source LLC
Chambersburg PA
CBHW080543290526
45790CB00006B/2536